Testimonials

Directors

"Thank you for "coloring our school" with enthusiasm, quality communication and an engaging learning environment."
~ Sylvie Robert, École Montessori Schule

"The Agility of Mind approach has fostered a positive learning environment with a desire to experiment and share motivating teaching practices between educators. It has been an enriching learning experience for all the actors of the community."
~ Lionel Carrara, Middle School Eau Vive

Educators & Trainers

"Sophie is able to give real concrete tools to be reused on a daily basis to learn better and above all, to understand learning mechanisms. This is the key to learning I think: knowing how WE function in order to make the best use of all our resources to progress. Sophie is both professional and very human."
~ Céline Gagey

"Sophie has a great ability to take the thinking to a higher level. She brings her pedagogical expertise with her usual energy, fun and friendliness."
~ Nadège Ravoux

Feedback Collected From Programs

"All of this should be taught as a priority to all teachers."

"Generalizing this training into elementary and high schools would be useful."

"Can't wait till next time, because there will be a next time!"

"Thank you so much for all the positive things you've done for us. Your good mood, optimism and ideas were, and still are a, breath of fresh air this morning."

"It was an enchanting experience."

"I go back to my copies, refreshed by the idea that behind each of them is a colour."

Students

"Thank you again for your help! It helped me regain my self-trust. What really worked for me, I think, was the 'Get Better' mentality and not the 'Be Good' mentality."
~ Joseph, 18 years old

"Sophie's method is really beneficial as, at the start, I was rather uncomfortable, unsure and stressed out frequently. After all of those sessions exchanging with Sophie, I felt much calmer and relaxed. Three sessions were sufficient to reduce my stress and helped me regulate myself much more with tips and exercises, thank you Sophie for everything!"
~ **Student, 13 years old**

Parents

"It is a magnificent work that is essential in building young people, in their capacity to know themselves, in their self-confidence and undeniably in their future success whatever path they choose to pursue."
~ **Rudi Bringtown**

"It is very rewarding to have this approach for our children. We think it's really great to work this way with them. How lucky they are to learn all of this now!"

How to turn children
into engaged learners

Copyright © 2021 Sophie Le Dorner

All rights reserved. No part of this publication may be reproduced, distributed, or transmitted in any form or by any means, including photocopying, recording, or other electronic or mechanical methods, without the prior written permission of the publisher, except in the case of brief quotations embodied in critical reviews and certain other noncommercial uses permitted by copyright law.

First published in 2021 by Hambone Publishing
Melbourne, Australia

Editing by Mish Phillips and Alexandra Wight
Book design and layout: Sadie Butterworth-Jones
Cover design: Ellen L. Caangay

For information about this title, contact:
Sophie Le Dorner
contact@sophieledorner.com

ISBN 978-1-922357-22-9 (paperback)
ISBN 978-1-922357-23-6 (ebook)

Contents

Acknowledgements i
About Sophie v
Preface vii
What to Expect xxi

PART 1: SHARING MY THOUGHTS 1

1: The Emotional Energy Matter 5

2: Engaging Interactions 13

3: Call to Action Through Interactions 21
First Interaction 25
Second Interaction 35
Third Interaction 40

4: A Common Language: How to bring trustful interactions together? 49
Curious and Agile 53
Mindful 62

5: Facilitating Learning 69
What does it look like when interactive learning has stopped? 76

How can we move the learner to a more positive emotional state? 80
A Whisperer as Facilitator 81
Ecology of Mind 85
Fertility of Time 90

6: Learning Experiences: An Iterative Learning **93**
Learning through Experiences 94

Part 1: In a Nutshell 103

PART 2: THE AGILITY OF MIND 107

7: A Caring and Engaging Environment which Relies on Interactions 109

8: Consciousness: Go Forward 113
Identify Your Teaching Preferences 113
Identify Your Learning Preferences 115
Create Colourful Pedagogical Capsules 117
Learning Phases 122

9: Connection: Connect With the Learners 125
Remote Obstacles 125
Active Listening and Feedforward 127
Positive Emotions 128
"Projection" 131

10: Curiosity: From Teaching to Facilitating 135
Activate Mind, Body, and Heart 143
Iteration and Collaboration 144

The Power of Questioning to the Development of Critical Thinking 145

11: Confidence: From Concentrating to Success 151
Focus Attention 151
Boost Memorization (a Complex Encapsulation) 154
Facilitate Comprehension 158
Stimulate Reflection (Thinking Back) 160
Liberate the Imagination 163

12: Communication: From Sharing Strengths to Everybody's Success 167
A Sustainable Ecosystem 167
Create a Constellation of Support 169
Multiply Interactions 169

Part 2: In a Nutshell 177

Summary 183

Acknowledgements

Deepest gratitude and lots of thank yous to all the wonderful friends, learners, and acquaintances I have met who have shared so much with me, provided me with useful feedback, and helped me through the process.

I call them my "Angels on the Side" and I have so many of them that I shall need a lot more than only a page, but here are a few: To my friend Lynn who has been a "cognitive and emotional doula"; Angie, for helping me make sense of my thoughts in English; Marjorie, for inviting me to re-imagine my thoughts; Céline, for being an amazing training partner; and Andrew, who has shared so many valuable thoughts with me. Lastly, Carine Chisu, another "thought leader buddy," who has helped me craft complex ideas into simple ones.

Thank you deeply to Brigitte Boussuat for sharing her fantastic approach and giving me some great feedback. Thank you to Thought Leaders, an extra-ordinary learning "tribe of chiefs" that showed me the way to self-trust with amazing insights. Thank you to Marie Legrand, who initiated a collaboration with me and gave me the energy to publish this book. Thank you to Geneviève Donea for her support in my practice. Thank you to Axipixi for offering some pieces of her wonderful drawing talent.

Thank you to Mrs Henriksen, Mrs Cuzziol, Mr Richard, Mrs Soekov,

Mrs Régniez, Mr Carrara, and Mrs Robert, who believe in my program, collaborated with me on so many levels, and enabled me to launch my approach in their schools. Thank you to the editor's team for helping me shape this book. I couldn't have done it without you.

A special thank you to my husband, who has always given me so much support every day and in so many ways, and my children Simon and Issao, who have always made me think outside the box and who fill me with joy and love every day. To my mother, who has shared with me a passion to learn through kindness and curiosity.

About Sophie

Sophie Le Dorner is an educational consultant, trainer, coach and speaker. She works internationally with organisations that are committed to creating a mindful and agile learning culture. She has built her strong international educational experience from working within schools, universities, and the French Ministry of Foreign Affairs.

Few educators have worked on as many different levels, with as many different parts of the education system. Whether it's directly with students, with family units, classrooms, school programs, or with the administration, Sophie's educational style is inclusive and exploratory. In particular, she specialises in building a learning culture through an Agility of Mind approach for educational organisations and companies.

Her mission is to adapt in a changing world, to learn and teach, and to train new generations of eager learners to do the same.

You can find Sophie at
https://www.sophieledorner.com
Contact@sophieledorner.com

Preface

"Sharing is sometimes harder than giving."
~ Mary Bateson[1]

The concept of *engaging in a learning journey* when sharing knowledge has been at the forefront of my mind since I started training, and then as a mother. I kept asking myself: What would be the best way to engage in learning today? If you have been asking yourself this question, we're on the same page! The desire to find an answer returned to the forefront of my mind with a child's smile and a hug after he completed a *Learning How to Learn* session that I had given at the European School II in Luxembourg. The student, at the end of his primary class, shared some whispered words: "Thank you, I didn't know my brain could do this! I feel I can do anything now." That day, I realized this child had touched me just as much as I had been able to engage him in the learning process, and consequently transform him through this experience. But how did this happen? How and why did he engage in this particular session? And what about the other children?

As a child I began my own learning journey aspiring to be a spy in order to master languages and create new identities. Like a spy, I wanted to be able to change and adapt each time I entered a new environment. I

---

[1] Mary Catherine Bateson was an American writer and cultural anthropologist (December 8, 1939–January 2, 2021)

wanted to connect with people and blend in as a chameleon. My desire was to travel and work in different parts of the world; I was aiming to understand what engages people and how to break communication codes. When traveling around Europe with my parents, I would try to create a perfect "cover" by mimicking and repeating words and sentences, as well as observing and listening to foreigners as much as I could. I was always intrigued by the way we could misinterpret a gesture, a behaviour, or even a shared language. I decided to study languages because I have always been interested in connecting with different people from different cultures, who all have different stories to tell. I was attracted by the intercultural aspect of sharing understanding through a common language, believing that we could find a common ground by looking at resemblances rather than differences.

I saw, in teaching French as a foreign language, the possibility to learn from the learners, as well as from the diverse topics themselves. Since I could teach through a variety of topics and in different places, I discovered *sharing knowledge* within companies and educational contexts in seven different countries, as well as teaching business French, literature, science, and phonetics. For me sharing knowledge has taken place both through training in companies and teaching at schools. I wanted to take the best of both worlds and bring the way we train in companies to schools. But I knew I needed some kind of data from numerous sources to develop an overall picture of the path or strategy to take.

To fulfil this dream, I became an Alice in Wonderland learner, constantly inquiring in order to create a global picture of what *engaging in learning* could look like. I became more and more passionate about the thinking process and developing my thinking skills through the theory of knowledge: *How do we know that we know?* The theory of knowledge courses from the International Baccalaureate[2] curriculum helped me explore knowledge questions and the eight ways of knowing: sense perception, reason, language, memory, intuition, faith, imagination, and emotion. Emotions are considered a way of knowing in the theory of knowledge and are omnipresent in all learning activities. But one day, after digging further into the learning process, I realized that emotions also have the potential to facilitate acquisition (e.g., perception and attention), storing (e.g., episodic memory and implicit learning), and use (e.g., decision-making and reasoning) of knowledge.[3]

When I heard of the definition of *engagement* in consumer neuroscience it all made sense to me, in this world of distraction we live in: Engagement is attention to something that emotionally impacts you and leaves a memory trace. It became obvious to me that emotion was at the centre of learning; therefore my goal became to find a way, through this emotional connection, to light a fire within learners.

The *how* we engage in learning has been lighting me up all these years, but I was just realizing it as I settled in Luxembourg. How can we create learners in an active learning arena who are eager to participate, willing to expend effort, and who can be motivated and inspired? I studied and practiced *engagement* internationally and in a number of diverse settings; after some years, I felt I needed to dig deeper into the *how we learn and life skill* matters in connection to neuro pedagogical

---

2   The International Baccalaureate offers an education for students from age 3 to 19, comprising of four programmes that focus on teaching students to think critically and independently, and how to inquire with care and logic.

3   LaBar & Cabeza, 2006; Lerner et al., 2015; Pool et al., 2016

approaches. Spying had caught up with me.

One day, after a conference I had given in Luxembourg on the subject of *Learning How to Learn* at home, a father and former head of training and development came to me and said, "Your presentation was funny." I didn't know whether or not this was positive feedback! So I asked him to develop his thought. He asked me if I knew Brigitte Boussuat and her approach to learning. I was intrigued. She has developed two approaches by combining social, emotional, and cognitive learning into two methods: pedagogical and behavioural. How clever! I felt I could finally join some dots together.

Boussuat's theory was an eye opener, but the approach that really transformed me, my thinking, and my behaviour is the one from Antoine de La Garanderie: it gave me clear processes as to how to learn, as well as an authentic humanistic approach to mediating knowledge. I had to change my behaviour from within: from delivering content to creating interactive experiences, and creating connections and dialogues within the learning arena.

All through my educational career I have worked with amazing educators who became disappointed by the world of teaching because of the need for quick and constant adaptation, the lack of resources, and student attention dropping in the classroom, as well as heavy admin tasks taking over their teaching jobs and no concrete ideas to help mitigate the everyday chores of their job that take so much time. The difficulty of differentiating students in a class of 20 to 30 children, with educators doing their best to bring passion and curiosity to the classroom in a limiting system, can quickly become overwhelming.

Preface

There are amazing educators who are downhearted because the new theoretical teaching ideas are not easy to implement in the classroom or, alternatively, take too long to implement effectively. The question that has often been raised is: How do we share responsibility with parents and balance expectations transparently to measure efforts meaningfully in the learning engagement of the child?

So many parents experience a fear about how little content knowledge their children will potentially acquire because of "their lack of interest or engagement" in most subject matters. I have also had parents share with me their difficulties in interacting with their children or their child's lack of perseverance. I am often asked, "How can I help my child to engage with their studies?" I have also often been told by children that they wish they could spend more time playing games or watching videos, rather than learning at school. Children tell me how bored they can be at school and that the only part they like is to be with their friends. They tell me that they are being told what to do and wish they could learn differently, through what they like instead. I have witnessed the impact from many educators who have engaged and connected with children, but the question I am often asking myself is: Are we really preparing them to fulfil their full potential?

As an educator and as a trainer, even in the most innovative places I have worked, I found a blend of simulative, creative activities but also painstaking struggles within the educators' teams: group work doesn't necessarily engage children any more in their learning and differentiation is often hard to put in place within a classroom. The Gallup Student Poll surveyed nearly 500,000 students from early childhood to secondary education in more than 1,700 public schools in 2012. They found that nearly 8 in 10 elementary students who participated in the poll were engaged with school, but by middle school that falls to about 6 in 10 students, and by high school, only 4 in 10 students qualify as engaged.[4] At school, instead of serving the children, instead of creating an engaging environment, I feel that we are imposing on the student whatever content we have to teach, independent of their desires and needs. At home, parents who decide to help their children in their learning journey also struggle to study with them. How can we bring engagement when children don't rely on the content, when parents don't always know how to help, and when educators are struggling?

We live in a rapidly changing world where the entire education system is constantly challenged by new knowledge and know-how. School drop-out rates are increasingly high on the educational landscape. While educators are required to adapt to find ways to engage children, they also need to lead them smoothly towards autonomy. Autonomous learners are motivated, self-directed, responsible, self-aware, and independent. They can also show awareness of some behaviours that reflect positively on their learning and this needs to be developed and practiced by educators. As my colleague Andrew Mowat[5] said to me, educators are *brain changers*, and they play a central role in a child's life. They are the architects of transformation, true leaders who can bring so much to children.

---

4   Brandon Busteed. (2013). "The School Cliff: Student Engagement Drops With Each School Year". Gallup Organisation, January 7. Available at: https://news gallup.com/opinion/gallup/170525/school-cliffstudent-engagement-drops-school-year.aspx

5   Andrew Mowat, trainer, coach, mentor in metacognition, leadership and courageous conversations expert.

Preface

Over the past year due to the global impacts of the COVID-19 pandemic, how to teach and learn has been flipped upside down. Many educators have been incorporating new tools in their lessons and students are experiencing new methods of learning. With this transition, it has become clear that with the required physical distance between educators and students, it is essential to find ways to connect with students and keep them engaged in the classroom and beyond.

Parents and caregivers have found themselves helping students navigate their lessons, while balancing their own responsibilities. This required developing extensive and new ways of communicating with students and families. The role of parents is pivotal for successful learning, but parents are adapting too and need guidance for their children. The role of parents remains essential for a child's full development in their schooling. More than ever, educators and parents must find new ways to keep learners attentive, to involve them, to give them the means to succeed while calmly leading them towards independent learning. Children who can develop independent learning skills at a young age can apply these to many areas of learning and life. It is not about stopping to support children as parents, but about stepping back and allowing children the opportunity to problem-solve and tackle challenges independently. It is only by doing this that we get a true understanding of what the child knows and is capable of.

As children start to take ownership of their learning and experience success, they develop invaluable confidence and self-motivation. This is the best present a parent can give to a child: showing them what their strengths are. Therefore, it is important to learn how to create a sustainable partnership between parents and educators to develop an attentive, agile, and caring learning approach in the ways we can best support children. Giving the best of one's self is what everyone tries to do, starting with the learner. "Who has met a happy failing student?"[6] Every child wants to succeed. Every parent has a dream of seeing their child reach their full potential. Every educator wants to motivate students, to keep them attentive, to make their teaching as effective as possible. And yet, on both sides, there are so many disappointments, breaks in the parent-educator dialogue, and students who drop out, facing life-long consequences.

As a former educator, the more I wanted to create engagement for learners, the more energy I needed to deliver content. I had the impression that being an energy source to engage them was the only way to captivate the learner. I would often be hit by a wave of exhaustion and a sense of discouragement. I had to be both creative and full of energy at all times but I also needed time and space to breathe. I wanted to share my knowledge to enable my learners so that they could transfer their new pieces of knowledge and move to the next wave, but I had the impression I was doing all the swimming. I know I am not alone in this feeling. When teaching adolescents, online or in class, I felt like I needed to always be in a high energy zone to compensate for my students' low energy. I had to learn to be okay with the silence and the mellowness of a class, in order to make the high energy special. Also, I had to give learners the opportunity to talk and give their energy to the moment, taking time to connect and synchronize with them rather than running through task after task. It is indeed the same when

---

[6] Marie Legrand, Ph.D., former teacher, trainer and speaker, author of "Libérer l'imagination" and "Apprendre en couleurs".

teaching adults; finding a balance is what it is all about for the learners, as well as for our own well-being. The energy diffuser is also important with parents' communication and administrative tasks. I remember an incredible colleague at the Australian International School who one day decided to help me all evening and showed me the way to be anticipatory versus reactive. She opened my eyes towards two concepts: ask for help and ask students to help you to keep your energy up.

Learning is not just about content delivery; it is a personal transformation and most educators know that. The more we learn, the more we change our brains. As learners, the understanding of new knowledge is theirs; it emanates from within. I realized that sharing knowledge should not only be a content-based experience but also an introspective quest, starting from the learners and not the content. I understood that listening to the learners was indispensable and the action of sharing knowledge needed to be created from them and with them, not imposed on them. I hoped to be able to enable them to learn anything and find their own ways of learning, to unlock their vast potential. I wanted them to dive into any topic, be happy to learn, and be successful. More and more, we need to help learners make sense of the world around them, deal with change, and learn new things while preserving their mental balance. For me, an important part of being an educator is being a learning designer: someone who can create a safe and engaging environment for learners to connect with themselves, as well as the material, and therefore bloom.

I have been in pursuit of developing an agile (adaptable) and mindful approach of my own to see how this could be replicated within the ecosystem of learning. At some points, I questioned whether my big vision of sharing the same system at home, at school, and online was realistic, or was I just pursuing a mirage? I found myself wondering if it would be possible to find a process that would work across home and school without adding work for the educators or undermining their teaching job. The parents' job is not to be teachers at home but to support their children in becoming confident lifelong learners, and to do this the parents need some learning keys to allow their children to learn with an agility of mind.

How can we share a visible learning model that will help parents and educators partner to engage learners at home, at school, or even online? Parents at home have always had to guide children in their learning and even share knowledge with them. Educators have always had to partner with parents to find the best strategies for learners to release their potential. What about starting with a positive dialogue between educators and parents by sharing a transparent way of learning? What about starting with questions about how the child can discover more about their strengths and preferences, rather than problems as a learner? I see educators as leaders, leading change in the classroom as well as shaping and sharing a vision within the community. When educators are leaders, they are committed to helping others achieve their potential. To achieve potential, the learning needs to be guided by a leader who observes the learning and encourages learning from an exploring place, rather than a fearful place of mistrust. Educators have knowledge of their subject, and sharing this knowledge can be done through experiential explorations. Parents and educators, hand in hand, can help the child explore this together by being both observers and actors through interactive dialogues.

Parents and educators share a common ground: they both have the same willingness to engage the child in their learning. Indeed, children are what connects educators and parents, but this new generation is very different from us (if you were born in the 70s like me!). So, what defines those young learners?

Young learners of today are being shaped in a context and time that is unique from what went on in our past. They embrace technology, and they are more practical and idealistic. They want to make a difference in the world and have purpose in their lives, but not necessarily a purpose in their jobs, except financial security. They love to switch from task to task, and have a high level of agility that helps them react to constantly changing environments. They are self-learners and have a healthy sense of curiosity, with access to and understanding of the tools that help them pursue their interests and find information quickly.

We are all living in this digital age, but the difference is that we didn't live through it in our formative years. 86% of young learners will be expecting more flexible working conditions, 78% will be more resilient, and 69% will be more reserved about face-to-face interaction.[7] This most recent generation is the connected, click 'n' go generation. They are living the "digital integrators" experience, with touch screens and a kinaesthetic learning approach to technology. They are highly digital and can watch 4 to 7 hours of screen time per day. For them, advice comes from experts and social validation. Their ideal leaders empower; they are enlargers who are capable of creating new leaders. It is a world of collaboration and co-creators.

---

[7] Mark McCrindle and Ashley Fell. (2020). "Understanding Generation Alpha." McCrindle Research, July. Available at: https://www.researchgate.net/publication/342803353_UNDERSTANDING_GENERATION_ALPHA

Young people will not only be looking for jobs but they will be creating their own jobs. This generation loves YouTube and social media videos in short snippets and easy-to-digest packages. More and more this generation is influenced by the heart and not the head or the content. A forecast for this young generation is that they may have up to six different careers. We often hear that this generation has a short attention span; I even remember my youngest child asking me why my text messages are so long. He informed me that he usually doesn't read them because he would rather have short words or emojis. This made me think and research: it is not that their attention span is shrinking but rather evolving to be more selective. This generation likes stimulating visuals, dialogue, and great stories, but not too many words. The ability to maintain focus may have actually improved over time, but this new generation chooses the content they consume. This short attention span helps keep the focus intense and narrative concise! The focus today seems to be more and more on learning and life skills for outcomes that would be more adaptable and entrepreneurial than employable. This generation doesn't have to wait for someone to give them an opportunity to make money, learn, create, or connect, since they can do so with people around the world, with resources on their devices. We therefore need to have all this information in mind when sharing knowledge online, at home, and at school. We need to think about how clear we are and show them what we want them to focus on.

Interest in this new generation made me reignite my personal learning journey, and I decided to commit to what this paradigm shift could really mean. I researched how an educator, a child, and parents and adults as individuals could share an engaging *language* that would be adaptive anywhere and at any time. Based on my practices and diverse interests, I follow, like Alice in Wonderland, the white rabbit wherever my curious mind brings me. I realized that my enthusiasm for learning was about to be fully immersed in learning and connecting with people in different areas in order to learn from them: neuropedagogy, behavioural and positive psychology, psychology of awareness as well as the discovery of the systemic approach. It was not only about learning the knowledge content but making sense of all of it and finding a way to make content more visible and interactive through the system. Imagining the process fuelled me with energy and passion. A vision of how to engage children was planted in my brain.

This book is an evolving piece of work that has been created through research, practice, and interactions with wonderful individuals, and this action-oriented philosophy will keep growing and evolving thanks to all of my future interactions.

One of the concepts most important to me in my work is that of 'interactions'. It's easy to let this word wash over you without really considering the significance of its two parts. Inter and actions. Both are equally important. Firstly, that it involves the relationship between two or more things. Secondly, that it requires actions. As you come across this word in the text, keep this deeper context in mind.

Today, I am sharing this living piece of learning at a certain moment in time and if you are like me, trying to find a way to engage, I invite you to capture whatever you feel and grow with it when it resonates with you. Join me on this journey...

What to Expect

Before sharing why thinking about learning as an ecosystem that connects home, school, and online is essential to engage children, first we will focus on emotions, in order to bring awareness to the essence of my approach. Once we understand the role emotions play in learning, we will delve into my personal beliefs about *interactive thinking and behaviours*. The next 10 years will need collective action to solve pressing problems that we all face, and to do this we need to harness collective learning. The application approach to learning today is no longer valid and we all know that. Yesterday's answers do not address today's questions. We need new questions and new answers: educators need to lead this learning transformation within the ecosystem of learners.

The second step requires re-imagining *sharing knowledge* in order to engage in learning. I will describe why sharing a common language allows us to reveal potential. After presenting the language of engaging interactions, step three will be dedicated to the facilitation of experiential[8] learning through the creation of questions. What are interactions and why are they so important? What forms of interactions are we talking about? Why do we need to create learning places that foster interactions and dialogue? Step four is about the *how* question. It will

---

8   Experiential learning is learning by doing. Professor D.A Kolb is the person most associated with experiential learning theory.

look at how we can create engaging learning and *true learning encounters* through dynamic and engaging dialogues, and experiential learning through an iterative approach. Experiential learning is putting into practice knowledge and skills by evaluating a child's learning. I will share a unique process that combines a philosopher's and educator's approach as well as a French behavioural expert's.[9] It will be a step-by-step quest that will foster interactions. This process is an intuitive global approach that will ease the way to learning for every member of the ecosystem. I will often use the word *learners* as a generic term since we are all learners in transition.

In **Part 1**, you will find more about my own personal thinking, the why and how to engage in a new way. **Part 2** will be more a mix of theory and practical actions that can be put in place in order to improve the process of engagement.

---

9   Brigitte Boussuat, author, speaker and trainer, founder of the 4Colors, 4Colors profile and Funny Learning as well as a network of 350 consultants.

TIME TO WONDER

To make this book a deeper interactive experience, I invite you to take out your pen and record some of your own thoughts as you read. If you need to exchange with a real person, consider dialoguing with a friend or a partner. You can also send me a message or share your thoughts with me: contact@sophieledorner.com

I believe in experiential learning (learning by doing) so let's start with a question:

If you had to share seven people who have touched you deeply and changed you in your learning journey, who would they be? And why?

PART 1
Sharing My Thoughts

Why does a child learn a language or solve a math problem? The reasons range from the intrinsic reward of having found the solution to getting a good grade, to avoiding punishment, to helping tutor a friend, to getting into a university, to pleasing parents or a teacher. All of the personal reasons for succeeding have a powerful emotional component and are connected both to pleasurable sensations and culture.

Students struggling with a math problem — or language learning — draw upon memories of past experiences with similar problems, searching for strategies that might also apply to this new problem. Essentially, solutions are found to problems that matter to us, and that are emotionally relevant to us. If the problem doesn't matter to us, interest is quickly lost. Attention wanders; learners disengage and begin to believe that learning is boring. If the grade matters, learners will often learn strategies for getting the grade without meaningfully learning the material.

For so many children, school environments are like a tsunami — something that just happens to them. Children become passive, weighed down with backpacks and expectations. Too few students experience education as something over which they exercise any meaningful power, or that has anything to do with their interests or needs. In their minds, school is boring or worse. However, guided by new ways of understanding learning, more learner-friendly environments and positive experiences can be designed for more students. Perhaps students can be engaged by encouraging them to take ownership of or power over their own learning. To understand how they can do that, we need to understand more about emotions first.

1
The Emotional Energy Matter

Emotional energy matter is at the core of this art of sharing knowledge, not only as a message but as a tool that allows us to use emotion to engage learning. For me, emotion and learning are inseparable. Emotion is the propeller for thought and the key to memory. I remember a 15-year-old child telling me that he didn't see the point of learning languages because, in a few years, robots would do it for him. Another child once told me that he couldn't be good at maths since no one was good at it in his family. As a child, I will always remember my last year of high school, my baccalaureate year and more precisely my final English oral exam. From the classroom where I was taking the exam, I could see that it was pouring rain outside and that the sky was grey. In a few minutes, I was about to be asked questions about a text I had had a few minutes to read. I was very anxious and worried I wouldn't be able to present my thoughts well enough. When the jury started to ask me questions, all I could hear was the harsh and distant tone of their voice, all I could feel was the stiffness of my body and shortness of my breath. I still remember how much I cried when the oral exam was over because I felt I hadn't been able to perform well.

This fearful moment didn't actually help me to share my knowledge. I had no tools to cope with stress and no idea that what was happening to me was also happening to others. I didn't know myself well enough to express my fear consciously and act on it. This is what many of our learners experience, because we tend to teach them content before teaching them tools to be in this world. Those everyday tools would actually be a pathway to better well-being, equity, and engagement. Lately, the humanity in people has been tested beyond limit and so, in response, educators need to create tasks that require the development of those daily skills and solve authentic problems that matter to learners at a deeper level for a more individual and collective well-being.

When I discovered *How Emotions Are Made* by Lisa Barrett,[10] it all made sense to me! She coined the theory of constructed emotion and explored the evidence that emotions are created spontaneously by several brain regions in tandem, and shaped by individual experiences. She explains that your brain is constantly predicting what sensory inputs to expect and what action to take, based on past experience. Then, when there is an incoming input, the brain either confirms its prediction or changes it. The brain creates an emotion by using prior experiences to predict and explain incoming sensory inputs (the effects are our general feelings throughout day) and guide action. Through this knowledge, it becomes clear that emotions are created spontaneously and based on individual experiences. They are not innate or fixed; instead, we construct emotions as architects of our own experience.

---

10   Lisa Feldman Barrett is a university professor of psychology at Northeastern University who focuses on affective science, and author of *How Emotions Are Made*.

We have a predictive system for the brain to keep the body running smoothly; it's called Interoception. The brain continuously processes internal and external sensations. The brain creates emotions through a complex system that also regulates the body's energy levels (our "Body Budget"). Emotion is a construction made by the relationship between culture, the brain, and our interpretations of our bodily sensations. Emotions are expressed by our predictions of what is happening around us. Emotions become behaviours and thoughts, to make sense of what is happening in certain contexts, either real or simulated. They produce thoughts about what we will do and whether to move forward or away from what has triggered the emotion. If emotion offers pleasure (social connection, hope, reward), learners usually approach learning peacefully; if it feels threatening (no sense of trust, not safe enough to speak up, too demanding, fear of disruption from other students) learners typically move away or try to make the threat move away. Emotions are at the centre of our decision-making and therefore our learning. People learn from their experiences and develop a range of actions that allow them to respond appropriately to different situations and, as our social world becomes more complex, so do the situations we must deal with.

Emotion is the propeller of thinking, learning, and decision-making. Without the emotional processes, skills and knowledge cannot be moved from acquired to novel situations. Emotion is needed to acquire this knowledge in the first place in any sort of meaningful sense. Memorization and regurgitation are not enough to transfer knowledge; meaningful learning is about internalizing concepts and skills, and connecting them to emotional goals thanks to emotional thinking.

Relevant motivation is *e.motion*: facts + practical understanding + feelings. E.motion is meaningful learning: motivation, purpose, and engagement, because it makes the learner move and it adds *motion* to the learning — these are the qualities most teachers long to see in their students. Educators love what they teach; it is important to them. On the other hand, what matters to the learners rarely finds its way into the classroom. This e.motion brings meaningful learning to the learner: it has a goal and is relevant to acquire knowledge. Emotion is either the *preparation* to action (e.motion) or inhibiting action. When an emotion is positive, we can move towards lifelong learning momentum.

But how could we use e.motion when there is a classroom with 30 children in it? Some educators connect to the emotional relevance of their subject through many innovative ways and others through being caring individuals. Yet the system does not seem to be succeeding. Too many students are dropping out, too many learn too little, and too many educators become frustrated, anxious, or too exhausted to try something new. A new understanding of the brain can help educators change practices in their classroom, but I can very well understand why some educators don't feel like implementing this new understanding: because it seems as if it is a very small repair when so much needs to be done to the system itself. However, something needs to change, and emotional relevance needs special attention from both educators and learners.

Emotional relevance can have many sources: curiosity, or the discovery of a new idea, or the enthusiasm of a parent or an educator. However, we must also consider that schools would be more successful if they were truly conceived and structured to nurture students' curiosity and encourage them to pursue their interests, connect their studies to their lives, or help them understand the world, as well as teaching them how to have healthy minds.

Social and cultural factors are as important inside the classroom as they are outside. If emotion is a propeller, it makes sense to help children learn to *steer their own way* and perhaps share William Ernest Henley's claim: "I am the master of my fate: I am the captain of my soul."[11] Wherever learning happens, it is not a rational or disembodied process; neither is it a lonely one. Learning is intertwined in our social relationships and our cultural context. We learn alone but also with people: educators, classmates, parents, and so many others. We always evolve within an ecosystem. We can't leave emotions at the door to clear the way for rational thinking. Schools need to be rethought not as *rational hermitage* but as interactive hubs of emotional thinking.

---

11   "Invictus" is a poem written by William Ernest Henley in 1875 and published in 1888.

TIME TO WONDER

But how does an educator today use emotion in the classroom, or online, to enable engagement to happen?

How do you engage in your own learning?

What are your interests and what are your strengths?

2 Engaging Interactions

Forging emotional connections with learners and linking cognition and emotion have important effects on well-being, as well as learning motivation and achievement. Interaction is also the motor of learning and development, and therefore a key to improving education.

Consistent adult and peer support through positive interactions provides a good basis for an emotionally supportive learning environment for learners. To have positive interactions, you can greet young learners by name or make sure to encourage their effort rather than the outcome, make constant eye contact, and acknowledge appropriate behaviours. Another useful strategy is to ask about their hobbies and interests, so that you can reference their background knowledge when needed. Showing them how you respond to your own mistakes can be a powerful lesson as well. Bring your emotion and explain the behaviours you're modelling in how to deal with those emotions. Having a neutral tone of voice and facial expression to inform when the learner's response is incorrect helps to keep the level of anxiety down. Tell the learner what you want them to do and immediately positively reinforce the learner for demonstrating the correct behaviour. For many years, we have disconnected emotion and cognition as well as a sense of collective learning within the classroom or within the ecosystem. Today, young learners need empowerment and collaboration through continuous lifelong learning for improvement.

Young learners of this new era will not have one job or career for their lifetime, so they will need to reinvent themselves over and over again to be able to adapt each time they enter the workforce. Engaging learners as a community creates a growing, connected ecosystem that shares the same vision and goes in the same direction. Human connectedness is key to learning achievement, and this human connection is about creating interactions through a collective mindset of beliefs. Learning is emergent, like consciousness, so we need a conscious learning shift from a passive delivery to an interactive continuity. The global challenges we are facing today have a complexity that we have never faced before. Today's challenges are bigger, more complicated, and more global than ever before. It affects every nation, every person and aspect of our planet, and even beyond. Lately, with the pandemic, homes were turned into schools and parents had to hold the educators' space. Parents have been forced to transform their homes into remote classes and educators have had to teach online. In a way, learning has always been and will always be happening at home. Teaching online will likely continue in the future, and therefore we must be prepared for it. When a team of individuals share beliefs through unified efforts, challenges can be overcome and positive results can be achieved. Creating active learning interactions between *home* and *school* and *online* is becoming more and more essential to create a learning continuity and a learning tribe. We all need to become actors of change to grow engaged children together. It all starts with creating a *positive* and *warm atmosphere* before delivering content in the classroom, at home, or online.

During the pandemic, effective learning outside of school placed much greater demands on autonomy, a capacity for independent learning, executive functioning, self-monitoring, and a capacity to learn online. Creating this warm connection before delivering content online was also challenging because of the time constraint we were faced with. When teaching at school, those essential skills among all students should be the primary focus. Most educators (and parents as well) found it difficult for many reasons, but here are the challenges I saw creating the biggest barriers: how to engage children in their learning far from school, and how to communicate with them and their family to guide their learning. When we talk about engagement, every one of us has a slightly different definition in their mind. At school, for some educators, engagement means listening attentively, participating in discussions, turning in work on time, and following rules and directions. For others, it may be largely understood in terms of internal states such as enthusiasm, curiosity, optimism, motivation, or interest. Today, more than ever, we need to develop learners as human beings rather than finding as many ways, as fast as possible, to get the curriculum in learners' heads. We need to enable them to develop soft skills and intrinsic motivation to engage them into a learning community, with better equity.

Modern biology reveals humans to be fundamentally emotional and social creatures. As brains and minds support the relationship between emotion and learning, the problem is not only to deal with one's own self but also to manage social interactions and relationships. For me, engaging learning is emotional, cognitive, and behavioural. Whether it is in a formal or an informal environment, many factors are involved. There are many interactions taking place:

- A mindful interaction between cognition and emotion that brings thoughts and actions together and enhances an individual *curious mindset*.

- Interactions between individuals and a collective (peer-to-peer) that is about learning behaviour, strategies, and mentoring or coaching actions in an *engaging group environment* (mindful and agile).

- Interactions with others in the community at large are about agile communication and defining *Learning How to Learn* actions.

A difficult communication at home could disrupt learning at school; the belief that we can only succeed if we are born gifted could prevent success at school, at home, or later at work; perceiving only one way to learn is a belief that could also have negative impacts on learning engagement, in the entire system. I remember a child telling me that he couldn't be good at languages because his parents were not. He had real difficulty engaging with the learning material. There was neither an emotional interaction nor a cognitive one. Those beliefs are dangerous because they can often prevent important skill development and growth, as well as sabotage your health and happiness down the line.

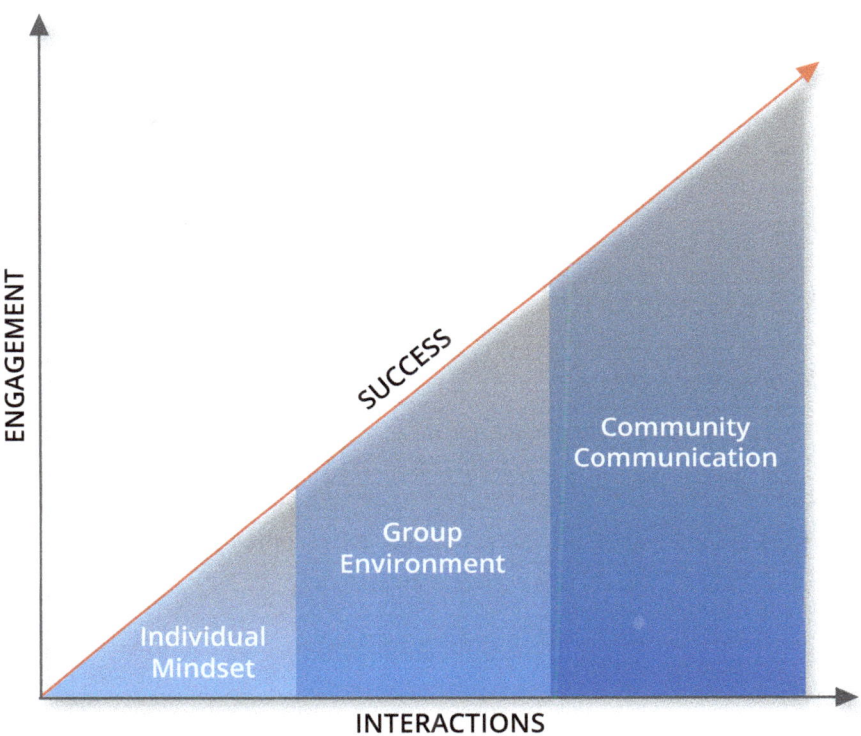

 # TIME TO WONDER

What impact does interaction have on learning?

More than ever, it appears essential to grow a sustainable ecosystem of learners connecting home and school, as well as online learning: What are your thoughts on this?

How can you help children to engage in a successful active learning journey?

3
Call to Action through Interactions!

Learners learn best when they own their learning through active engagement, clarity, and positive emotional exposures. Today, the world is evolving so rapidly that we feel insecure about what's coming next; the lack of an agile interactive process through the ecosystem prevents us from adapting individually and together. We know that the brain doesn't like uncertainty, and therefore this fear of change brings anxiety and worry, both of which can prevent us from reinventing ourselves. What if we could imagine a learning tribe that shared the same philosophy, "change for the better" or kaisen (a fusion of two Japanese words, *changes* and *better*) in which we could set up new habits, simplify study flow, reduce stress, improve outcomes, eliminate overly ambitious learning content, and motivate through positive energy. The energy you give off not only determines your interactions with other people, it also speaks about how you're feeling about yourself. The key action to have positive energy is to shift your mindset from "it can't be done" to "I can do it" or "we can do it." A positive and clear thought process and positive actions will bring trust within the learner and within the community. Thoughts, emotions and actions need to be well balanced to bring learning together.

To share the same philosophy, we would need clarity over content. The first time I heard of John Vervaeke's Agent-Arena Model[12] was when sharing ideas with Andrew Mowat. This approach has a deep place in interactions to better engage learners and focuses on two key aspects: the arena and the agent.

The arena is the location where the action occurs, such as how a football pitch is the place where the game is played. We often assume that parents, children, and educators know the arena they are playing in. However, an important step is to define this arena in order to organise actions and accurately calibrate achievement. Schools, classrooms, and homes are our arenas.

The agent aspect of this model is the person who acts in a certain way, such that their role helps to achieve the goal for themselves and the team. Being an agent is being capable of pursuing your goals, and organising your thinking and behaviour, so that actions appropriately fit the situation. Having a sense of *agency* is feeling in control of things that happen. Developing the capacity to engage strategically in the learning without waiting to be directed is a must today, so examining learner agency in your setting is an important reflection. What is

---

12   John Vervaeke is a professor of cognitive psychology and science at the University of Toronto. For more information about the Agent-Arena Model, see: https://awakeningfromthemeaningcrisis.com/agent-arena-relationship

the learner doing? What is the adult doing? What's happening in the environment?

Human beings are inherently social creatures: we are wired to be with others. When going through stress in our learning journey, a sense of human connection is one of our fundamental needs.[13] Social connection can lower anxiety and help us regulate our emotions. Feeling socially connected, especially in an increasingly isolated world, is more important than ever. We need the best of all insights to tackle difficulties and therefore learn through supportive relationships to frame a guiding purpose and identify actions to achieve a learning goal. We also know that when the brain learns, it creates new connections all the time and, therefore, the brain changes. As such, learning needs a shift of mindful awareness to create a self-correcting system which responds to changes positively and enables learners to fully understand their own selves, as well as each other.

---

13   Matthew Lieberman, social psychologist, neuroscientist, and author of the book *Social: Why Our brains Are Wired to Connect*

TIME TO WONDER

Human beings are trying to make sense of this VUCA world (volatility, uncertainty, complexity, ambiguity) but with all the facts we have today about this generation's urge to change the world, where do we start as educators?

Let's start individually by asking ourselves, why we do this job?

What changes do we want to see?

What is in our power in this world of uncertainty, meaning: what actions can we take?

First Interaction

This **first interaction** is between cognition and emotion, to enable us to grow into mindful and agile learning individuals and to create a curious mindset. Emotion and cognition have long been treated as independent entities, but it is now clearly understood that emotion and cognition are in fact highly interdependent. Therefore, thanks to active emotional and cognitive introspection on how we behave when learning and teaching, we will grow a powerful ability to learn and feel comfortable with change and mistakes.

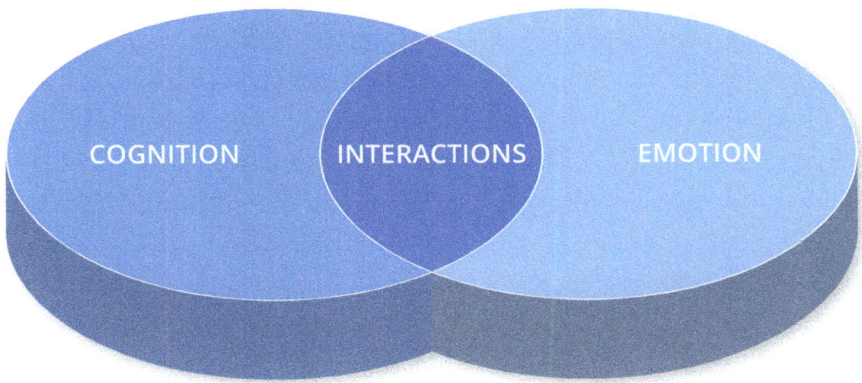

Learning has to do with what the mind produces as individuals, because only when information enters the mind in some form does it begin to make sense. Examining our own conscious thoughts and feelings is the process of introspection and it relies on the observation of our mental state. The goal of this active introspection is to gain emotional and cognitive awareness and become curious actors. This way of looking inward and examining thoughts, feelings, and actions is an experimental process. This process provides knowledge that can help people make connections between experiences and materials or experiences and responses. To trigger this first interaction, it needs to be an active mindful step into a curious mindset, linked to the idea of having a growth mindset.

When reading Carol Dweck's inquiry into our beliefs, synthesized in her book *Mindset: The new psychology of success,* we realise how fixed mindsets can sabotage behaviours and impact our learning engagement and improvement. Carol Dweck describes the difference between a fixed mindset and a growth mindset and how they impact a successful learning journey.[14] With a fixed mindset, learners believe that their basic abilities, their intelligence, and their talents, are just fixed traits. They have a certain amount of ability and after that their goal is to look smart all the time and avoid any circumstances that may make them look stupid. When students have a growth mindset, they recognise that although not everyone can be a genius, we can all develop our talents and abilities through effort, good teaching, and persistence.

We tell our children, "Wow, you're such a maths person, and your little brother is an artist" failing to see that whilst this fixed mindset reassures them in the short run, it hinders their long-term ability to learn, grow, and develop new skills (such as art or math). Your actions can change your beliefs, and with small, repeated actions, you can enable a growth mindset process to kick in. Plus, focusing on the process, and not the outcome, can cultivate skills.

---

14   Stanford University psychologist Carol Dweck wrote the ground-breaking *Mindset* in 2006.

It is important to become mindful of your own learning as an educator, as it is a great source of personal knowledge and reflecting on it in action can be a catalyst to enrich your students. Being mindful of our thoughts, environment, emotions, and actions prepares learners to be active and curious in their own learning. This can also lead to self-esteem, build self-management, and enhance interpersonal relationships. As we grow to being more mindful of ourselves, our interactions and our environment grow and enable us to engage more in learning. As we grow in our conscious mind, you may notice how fear stops the learning process from taking place. You may notice that fear is often present in the classroom: fear of not knowing, of not being good enough, of not having a good grade, or of appearing silly in front of peers. When we are trapped in this fearful emotion, we can't move forward and be curious.

I will always remember this 17-year-old girl at school who came to me and said, "Thank you for sharing with me how to stop my stress." For many years, she had thought she was not good enough because she couldn't perform well during her exams. She had no idea what was going on internally with her during tests, only that she might have a memory problem and therefore didn't want to get any help to discover the reasons for this emotional roller coaster, all because she felt so ashamed and alone. She told me how explaining the teenage brain and linking it to emotions helped her make sense of what was happening to her. I had shared the acronym from Daniel Siegel with the classroom (E-S-S-E-N-C-E), explained in his book called *Brainstorm: The power and purpose of the teenage brain*.[15]

---

15 Daniel J. Siegel M.D. is the author of *Brainstorm*, as well as *The Whole-Brain Child*, *The Power of Showing Up*, and many other books. He is a professor at UCLA, and executive director of the Mindsight Institute.

When I shared the square breathing technique, she even went further to discover more about how she could regulate her stress. This knowledge was how she overcame her stress and was able to release her potential. She went from having average grades to being above average. She felt more confident and wanted to try things by herself. She started developing the agility of mind through iterative processes with trial and error. She would ask herself what she did well and what she could improve upon. When we become more perceptive, and more present, we can become more creative and bring clarity to our learning.

Since no two brains are alike, we all learn best when we find our own answers in a more creative and non-directive way. This happens in the process of making new connections. The mind is logical, sequential, and procedural in one part and creative in the other part. In the unconscious part, we have automatic responses or habits, built for optimization or learning from past experiences, which allow us to drive without thinking about the action consciously. On the other side, the mind is built to learn new things more consciously; this part is wired to create and plan for the future, and for novelty. Interestingly, this part is also linked to happiness. Edward de Bono discovered in his research that insight (becoming aware of new information) is always linked to spontaneous laughter. It turns out that discovering or learning something new makes us happy. Learning with an agile mind is to explore the unknown as much as it is to link it to the past; to follow procedures and rules as much as creating new ideas and trying out new things.

For many years, I taught French without any knowledge of introspective inquiries. What I wanted was to teach French differently than how I had learnt it. I didn't want to teach through the delivery of grammatical theory; I wanted to teach grammar through examples. I believed that I was sharing my knowledge through an empowering approach, one that encouraged students to think of the how and why. But at that time I couldn't see that some of the students were puzzled and lost, I was so certain that it was the best way to teach. One day, I realised that it was my own way of learning and not everyone could be taught in the same way. This is when I decided to understand more about my own way of learning, become more mindful of learning differences, and open myself to other ways of learning to bring my teaching to the next level. I realised that I was fearful of not being able to teach the content and help learners engage with their learning. I had a fear of not knowing how to *fix* learning problems. A fear of giving away my knowledge power.

TIME TO WONDER

Here are 10 intuitive beliefs, confirmed by science, that can help you reflect on your own thinking and become conscious of your own thinking process.

What are your personal thoughts, feelings, and actions when you read the following statements?

Rank each one on a scale from 1—5, based on how aware you feel you are of each, with 1 needing the most improvement.

- [ ] I believe that everyone can learn.
- [ ] I know we use all of our brains, not only 10%.
- [ ] I think we use both the right and left brain.
- [ ] I teach in a multimodal way because there is no learning style.
- [ ] My teaching style is "less is more" (working memory is 2–7 chunks).
- [ ] I make breaks and space for learning.
- [ ] I link old information to new information for my learners in order to help it make sense.
- [ ] I celebrate effort as much as result.
- [ ] I create a trusting climate, which enhances learning.
- [ ] I enhance motivation and self-regulation through growth mindset versus a fixed mindset.

Enabling children to own their learning through mindful learning introspection is all about enabling them to find answers through their own thinking. When educators allow children to become aware of how their mind produces knowledge, children feel empowered and become more confident. This process is about building confidence between individuals and trusting children's capacities.

> *"In companies, when team members hold positive beliefs about the team's capabilities, there is greater creativity and productivity (Kim & Shin, 2015). And in schools, when educators believe in their combined ability to influence student outcomes, there are significantly higher levels of academic achievement."*
> **Bandura, 1993**[16]

One day, during one of my *Leaning How to Learn* coaching sessions, a 12-year-old child came to me feeling defeated because his motivation for learning Spanish had become extremely low. His mother had told me that she also noticed some repercussions in his other subjects as a result. I could sense this feeling of giving up, of "I can't do well," and "I am not good enough," all because of him not understanding anything in his Spanish class that day. Some months ago, I would have asked him what the topic was and then would have explained everything to him right away. But this time, I wanted him to feel the power of *I can do it*, so I said to him: "What did you understand?" When he answered "Nothing," I asked him to go back to that moment and tell me all about what he remembered about the video the teacher had showed him.

---

16   Jenni Donohoo, John Hattie and Rachel Eells. (2018). *The Power of Collective Efficacy*. Leading the Energized School. Vol 75, No 6, pg 40-44.

While he was telling me about it he said, "Oh, I see, those words are used in different spaces." He asked me, "Why?" I asked him to repeat the examples he had given me and I wrote them down. He suddenly had a big smile on his face and said, "Oh yes, it all depends on where things are located." By just letting him go into his thoughts, he connected the dots and felt empowered. I then asked him what he could do next time to make the links himself. He answered that he could explain it to someone in his own words. He understood that sharing his knowledge with a friend or a parent could help him translate his thoughts and he realized he could understand much more than he originally thought. It made me feel so happy that day when I heard this child say to his mum, "I can learn Spanish, mum."

Preventing learned helplessness[17] behaviour in the classroom is incredibly important work that educators need to focus on. When experiencing this helpless feeling of negativity, children can become more likely to learn that they shouldn't try new things for fear of failure or rejection. I remember a time, in my second year of teaching middle school, when I was struggling to explain the French pronoun "on" and seeing the look on my students' faces that clearly meant: "What is she talking about? I can't do this." I could feel that students were puzzled and lost. Seeing this, I decided to give students a voice. I said to them, "Thank you in advance for your help because we can sometimes feel stuck. If you keep the thinking going by asking some questions, you can un-stick yourselves." I truly believe that by modelling that fearless response of not knowing, children will dare to ask questions, make errors, and embrace new knowledge.

---

17   Martin Seligman, father of positive psychology, educator, researcher, and author of several bestselling books including *Learned Optimism: How to Change Your Mind and Your Life*.

As an educator, modelling positive and exploratory learning is powerful. One key to preventing this learned helplessness in the classroom is adopting an exploratory approach. This must be done with a curious mindset created through awareness and trials that will engage children positively towards learning through an agility of mind. We must ask ourselves: Can we be ok with being temporarily ignorant?

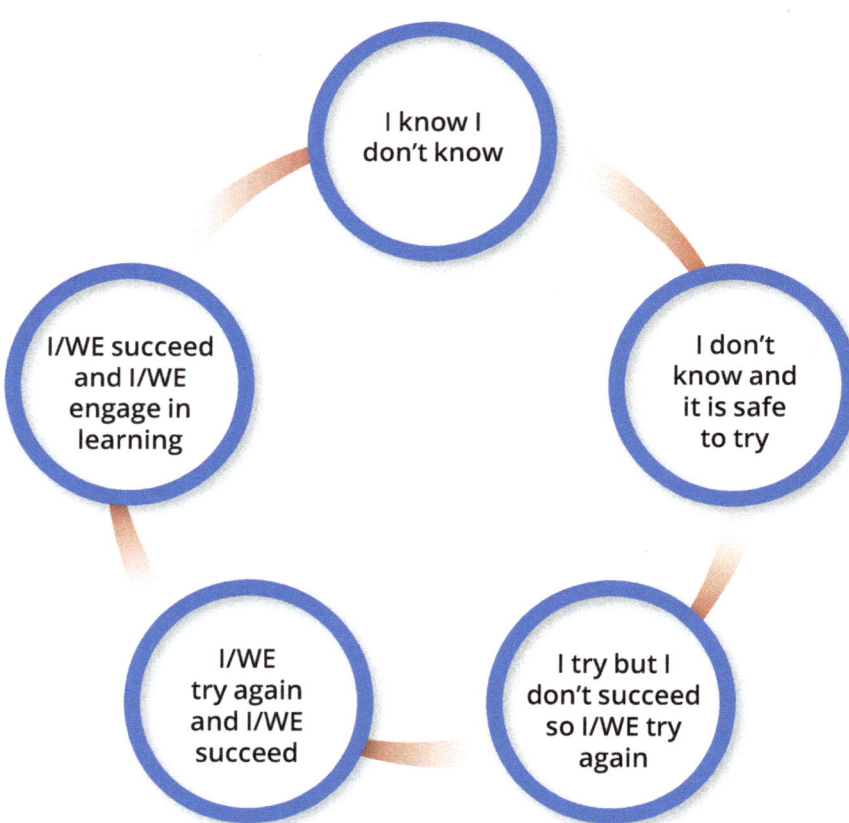

Second Interaction

The **second interactions** need to create engaging spaces between learners through *peer to peer* collaborations: content expert educators between content expert educators, children between children, mentors and children. I am tempted to call this part: learners interacting with learners.

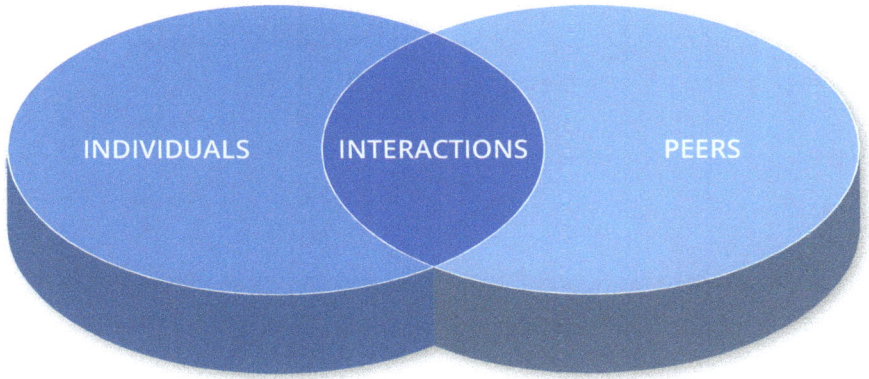

Before sharing any knowledge, having a connection between learners is essential to begin. To do so, I really enjoy the Powerful Questions Pyramid™[18], shown on the following page.

---

[18] Will Wise and Chad Littlefield, *Ask Powerful Questions: Create Conversations That Matter*, 2017

Before leaving the Australian International School in Singapore, a group of secondary students created a video for me as a goodbye gift. In this video, one young learner said, "You don't teach, you connect with your students." This sentence resonated with me for many months and I decided to dig deeper into the research: Why was this important for him and the other students who had told me the same thing? In *Ask Powerful Questions*, I was presented with the *Project Aristotle* research from Google about people achieving a high performance when there was a sense of personal connection. Relationship and connection are indeed the pre-condition for change, because without relatedness, no work can occur. I remember a math teacher sharing with me the fact that when working in the peer-to-peer program we had initiated together she had realized how much we needed this connection, and therefore had decided to utilize this in her own classroom.

Peer teaching can take many forms, but the common factor is that knowledge is shared not by another person but by people on the same *level*, teaching each other what they know. Learners share similar experiences and ask questions of each other, and that common experience has significant benefits because they understand the issues they each face on a more personal level. The level of insight in peer-to-peer interactions does wonders for learners. Not only does it build a connection based on trust and respect but it fosters learning at a different level. It is a win for everyone to reinforce knowledge and gain insights. Peer-to-peer learning also includes mentoring or problem-solving meetings.

When I was working in Edinburgh as course director, I remember putting a board on the wall of the educators' sharing room with a Sell and Buy Marketplace. This was a place where ideas could be shared and questions asked. When educators couldn't find answers, training would take place. In the last international school (Australian International School) I worked with, the same mentoring program allowed me, as an educator, to choose from three topics I was interested in and to connect with other educators to get relevant and practical information. This peer learning was more than I could ever have hoped for, and was all the more essential because it all made sense to me, leading me to feel inspired to take action. This is a simple resource that can be created in any school to help foster interaction and support educators in their workplace.

Professional development is essential in today's educational system because it continuously needs to meet the demands of society. Learning from and with peers is an effective approach to educators' development, and working together through trust and kindness, through peer coaching in a safe environment, is essential to the idea of mutual learning. Showing young learners that educators are supporting each other and still learning from each other is a powerful way to model lifelong learning. Peer to peer can also be teachers collaborating together: OECD studies show that higher-performing countries intentionally focus on creating teacher collaboration that results in more skilful teaching and strong student achievement.[19] U.S. researchers have also found that school achievement is much stronger where teachers take part in collaborative teams that plan and work together. According to Albert Bandura, when educators share a sense of collective efficacy, school cultures tend to reflect high expectations for student success.[20] John Hattie synthesized various influences in different meta-analyses in a groundbreaking study that showed that collective teacher efficacy was the most important factor related to student achievement.[21]

Focusing on student learning as opposed to instructional compliance can bring a shared language through actions. Educators become change agents when they collaborate. When they believe that it is fundamental to evaluate the effect of their practice on their students' progress and achievement, they also believe in finding solutions of efficient practice together.[22]

Peer to peer, between children, consolidates learning by allowing them to review their own learning, increasing their confidence and

---

19 Linda Darling-Hammond, "Teaching and Learning International Survey," 2014.

20 Albert Bandura is a Canadian psychologist and professor from Stanford University.

21 John Hattie, "Collective Teacher Efficacy," 2016.

22 Hattie & Zierer, 2018

developing communication skills, and could also be used to assess learning based on their ability to share their knowledge with a fellow peer. I remember Col Fink[23] telling us in a mentoring webinar how explaining the course content to a classmate helped him become aware of what he really understood. This memory of him as a child allowed him to realise how important those experiences of exchanges are, and how they consolidate learning. Relationships with peers are important for children's development, in terms of personal, social, and emotional aspects of development.[24] There is evidence that peer interactions, and the general social climate of the classroom, affect both school engagement and a learner's academic achievement. Moreover, based on the works of Piaget and Vygotsky, educational psychologists consider that children's interactions are pivotal for cognitive development. A vast majority of students claim that their fellow peers have influenced them immensely and positively in their studies and social behaviour.

In the ISEP intercultural program online (a non-profit organization that partners with 300 universities around the world) I worked on recently, Cédric Guern (ISEP coordinator from Caen University and ISEP chair) and I discussed how to bring social learning/interactions to online training. We thought of creating a third session with students sharing experiences with other students to bring interactions together. When working in Laos for the National Organization for Studies in Politics and Administration (NOSPA), learners had created a weekly newspaper in French and had a very important action: working together as a team to

---

23   Col Fink is an Australian-based thought leader and author of *Speakership* and *Tribe of Learning*.

24   Kindermann, 2007; Skinner & Bemont, 1993

share some pieces of information about politics in Francophone countries. This newspaper, called *FrancoLao*, was distributed in the French Embassy as well as the French Institute which made this approach very concrete to the learners.

For children, as for adults who are willing to learn from each other, a constellation of support and accountability buddies could be created to move forward, take responsibility, and act upon. When supporting each other, resilience[25] is strengthened and the ability to bounce back after stressful situations is empowered. Recently, through miro.com, I created a special action plan for an adolescent boy who asked me to support him in his studies. Only through his trust and our interactions could I have managed to create these action plans, because he was the only one who could make the choice to learn. Trust is the glue that can make peer to peer or mentoring programs occur: a desire to learn and not to blame, honest and authentic dialogues, and an atmosphere of enjoyment, openness, and transparency are necessary.

Third Interaction

As such, the **third interaction** would be a trusting partnership within the ecosystem. An ecosystem can be described as a community network of interactions between organisms and their environment. If we see a school as an ecosystem, we realize how every element of a school affects other parts. Parents, teachers, and caregivers are all part of this system and positive interactions between these parts will create balance for an individual's growth and learning. Trust is a crucial factor to create

---

25 This term was used for the first time in 1626 and today, in positive psychology, a resilient person works through challenges by using personal resources, strengths, and other positive capacities of psychological capital.

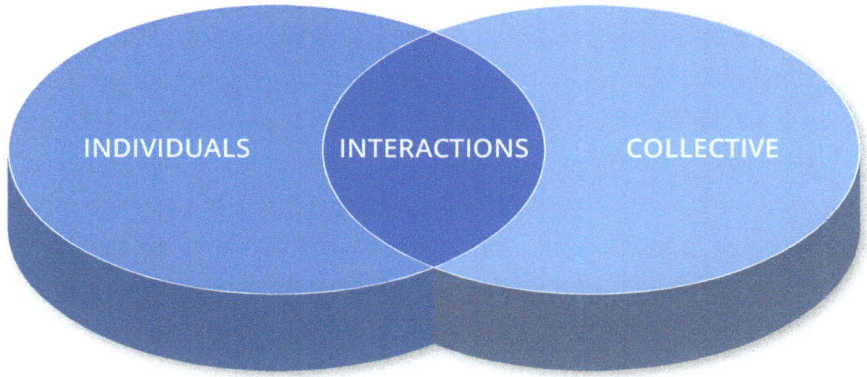

this balance, and even more so in relationships between parent-educators and their children. It has been established that trust generally enhances parental involvement in school and their interactions with educators, as well as their children's educational achievements.[26] Trust as a dynamic disposition and attitude gives learners the ability to take action. Educators and parents provide a vital support system to help young learners flourish. Both groups are important. When parents and teachers have good communication and can work well together, it can significantly impact each student's long-term success.

When I was studying in the USA, I had a teaching internship at a primary school. The first thing that I was asked to do was a video presenting myself to the parents. Who was I? What was it I wanted to do this school year and how was I going to do it? Co-creating a partnership through clarity and connection was my goal and this was to

---

26   Adams & Christenson, 1998; Beycioglu, Ozer, & Sahin, 2013; Janssen, Bakker, Bosman, Rosenber, & Leseman, 2012; Mitchell, Forsyth, & Robinson, 2008; Tschannen-Moran & Gareis, 2015.

create a trusting environment, showing how much I would value help and insights from the parents. This video was my first approach to creating a partnership with parents. My project was to create a positive classroom environment and support children to engage in their learning. This also included examining ways in which parents and families could encourage, motivate, and reinforce children's learning at home, examining links between home learning activities and learning in the classroom; exploring how the family could also be involved in the classroom; providing tips for families on schoolwork activities monitored at home; involving students' progress between home and school; and involving families in setting student goals each year. Those same type of recordings could also be done by the students in class and sent to parents. To learn to communicate in an agile way, I discovered a tool that made me understand the different ways of engaging with parents and it will be shared with you further.

All the members of the system are interconnected, so the loss or change of one factor can have large ripple effects through the entire ecosystem. As a society, we depend on healthy ecosystems to do many things: to purify the air so we can breathe properly, cycle nutrients so we have access to clean drinking water, and pollinate our crops so we don't go hungry. If your being depends on each other's actions, you are thus responsible for those actions and their consequences. The African saying, "It takes a whole village to raise a child," comes into play here. From a psychological point of view[27] the child benefits from having multiple inspirations and feeling secure to explore and learn in

---

27 According to Todd M. Trash and Andrew J. Elliot, inspired individuals were more intrinsically motivated.

3: Call to Action through Interactions!

a loving environment. We have looked at learning in a disconnecting way, behaved in an increasingly independent manner, and designed learning without inspirational interactions. Collaborating towards a common goal in the global learning interest is essential today. We therefore have and need to define our global learning interest at home, at school, and online.

If success is the desired outcome at school for all children and, as a consequence, well-being, we need to define success. We may choose engagement through interactions as the key component of success. Success in the classroom could also be the ability to cooperate, to self-monitor, to set goals. Perhaps it is more a process, considered a starting point for each learner. Success is having the courage and confidence to learn when facing the unknown (a curious mindset) and it depends on a strong ability to know oneself and the ability to work with people. Success could be all the little things a person does to give others joy. Success could also be a connection to something larger than yourself. Success is like beauty, a subjective ideal that is different depending on who you talk to. So, success is not only about getting the best grades, but it is also about having children engage in a meaningful learning journey. Learners are therefore also successful when they are prepared to participate collaboratively in a learning community, as well as to learn from and contribute to the various communities they are a part of. Learning at this point requires human beings who can model humility, adaptability, and a nurturing attitude; as for learners, facilitating requires vulnerability, adaptability, and resilience.

In both cases, agility is the key to live a global learning life, but certainly not fear. This learning approach needs to connect the heart and mind to create an agile approach. An agile communicative approach that allows and encourages individuals within the ecosystem to grow together is helpful. The ecosystem of learners would support the learning process through different ways of thinking. An agile model in the practitioners' world would be action-oriented more than theoretical because it involves sharing continuous learning by using this approach. These interactions are crafted from the lessons of trying to cope with change in the face of complexity, so we start small, learn fast, and embrace mistakes. By carving out small actions, focusing on specific outcomes, and having a curious mindset, we can make a more open, iterative improvement. We need to celebrate the learning and new insights that come from learners' efforts.

Since a learning ecosystem is nothing without people, and a good *relationship* between people, it needs a set of principles to be aligned in the system to be as clear as possible.

For Franklin Covey, principles are self-evident; they affect human behaviour and interactions, which is evident historically speaking across cultures globally. Covey said, "A principle is a natural law like gravity. If you drop something, gravity controls. If I don't tell you the truth, you won't trust me; that's a natural law."[28] These principles determine the ultimate outcomes or consequences of behaviour and actions, in the same way as gravity determines that objects fall.

What about interaction principles within the ecosystem?

---

28   Franklin Covey, *The 7 Habits of Highly Effective People*, 1989

3: Call to Action through Interactions!

- Start with the learner's strengths and interests: we can all learn, so let's engage positively and trust learners' capacities.

- Listen, observe, feel, move, and think critically through questioning.

- Support each other and adapt to differences by creating clear agile structures that are easy to change little by little.

- Share knowledge through listening, clarifying, and having authentic communication with no judgement.

- Share visible *feedforward*[29] (a more positive way to approach feedback) and progress: making choices, patterns, and outcomes visible.

- Respect each other's time and space and accept differences in their own learning ways.

- Take pleasure in learning and embrace mistakes.

---

29 Feedforward is a concept originally developed by a management expert Marshall Goldsmith to avoid mental shutdown, to reinforce positive behaviour, and to focus on development rather than ratings.

TIME TO WONDER

What would your principles for a new visible learning solution between yourself, parents, and children be?

What are your goals according to these principles?

How would you define success in life and in school?

What do we want to pass on to young learners?

A Common Language

How to Bring Trustful Interactions Together

Knowledge cannot originate from a single entity or discipline. Effective and engaging learning needs to be interactive. I won't go into the interdisciplinary approach,[30] which is also an essential part of engaging in learning, but I will focus on creating an environment for communicative and pedagogical interactions that are key to learning transformation. Interactions are the seeds that will grow within the ecosystem. Interactions need three forms: mindful, curious, and agile. Those three words have been overused in a variety of settings but never put together to bring out the best meaning.

We know that parents are the provider of their child's education from birth through adolescence. Because home is the primary environment in which the child's potential and personality will be shaped it is

---

30   An approach to curriculum integration that generates an understanding of themes and ideas that cut across disciplines and of the connections between different disciplines and their relationship to the real world.

important to create a positive atmosphere that will not only support what goes on in the classroom but also instil the desire to learn. Building an effective relationship between the educator and the parent is a critical task, and everyone wants to achieve this goal. As with relationships, mutual respect and lots of positive communication are the foundation. Parents and educators can provide each other with unique insight and different perspectives. A successful engagement is an active partnership in learning, which, through a common language, enables learners to bridge their worlds: school, home, and online.

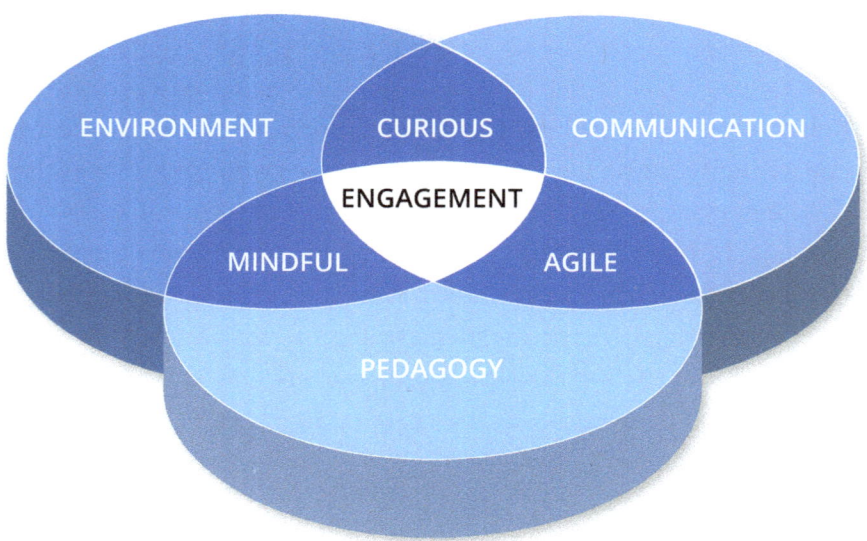

4: A Common Language

While presenting this common language at an online parent interaction conference at the École Montessori Schule Hobsheid in Luxembourg, a parent shared some questions that could be added to a document I had co-created with Lara, the educator. This truly became the highlight of the evening. I realised that by sharing a language, and opening up through a trusting conversation, true sharing could happen.

The common language of the ecosystem could be a subtle dose of agile communication and clear awareness of how we learn. "Sensing"[31] knowledge through a mindful approach when possible in order to bring awareness could be the *how* to start. What about embedding a pedagogical and communicative model that would bring two key components to the learning phase within the ecosystem: a *common language* through an experiential process that would connect us all as learners? I am using the word "language" at this point because language is the primary means for communicating ideas and emotions between individuals. Language is a process itself that brings continuity to the ecosystem. It is a collaborative device for communication, and then for synergy. Language itself is a behaviour for social purposes and it often evolves throughout our daily lives. Developing and expressing clear thoughts between people is essential to connect. This language is also knowing that our values, language models, and cultures are different for each of us. For that reason, it is crucial to check the understanding of what we mean and the other person means, without being surprised by it. We need to believe in every one of us and bring a sense of competence to children that is at the core of learning.

---

31   Claus Otto Scharmer is a senior lecturer in Organization Studies at MIT, founder and director of the Presenting Institute and author of *Theory U*.

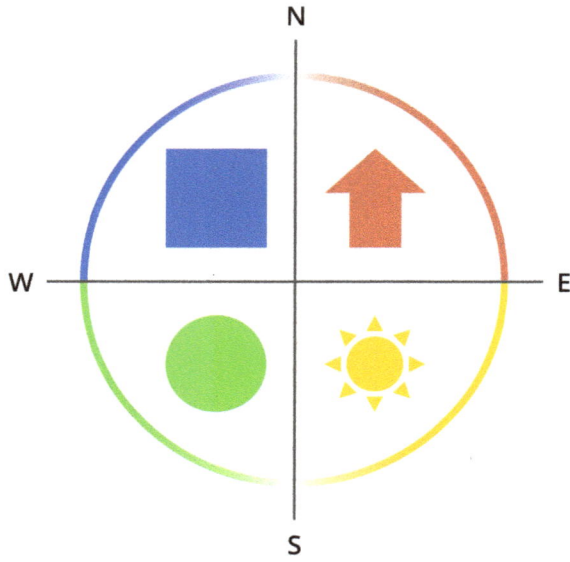

I had a call from a mother during the Covid lockdown, who felt that her 8-year-old boy was not as engaged as when he was at school. She was worried that he was lacking some learning motivation. When she realised that he just didn't know how to engage with the material, I shared with her the compass, a simple tool about *Learning How to Learn,* and we both cut the schoolwork into colourful chunks that her boy needed to do for the teacher. She used this compass at home and within 24 hours her boy succeeded in engaging with the material again. She was then able to show her son this strategy so that he could do it on his own, creating even more ownership over his own learning. This way, the child had a way to go through his learning routines. The pre-coded colour code by the mother helped the child to choose his steps. It was a brilliant experience for me because I realised that this approach could really be the language shared with parents.

Curious and Agile

We could be like detectives and use a lens to always be aware of our behaviour at school, at home, and online. For that, we would need a neuro behavioural and pedagogical approach that brings together the ecosystem and can be easily understood by everyone. The primary language could be the one of colours, by sharing a collaborative effort of self-organization and through teamwork in colours within the classroom; an intuitive model, a communicative, and emotional approach: the 4Colors®.[32] The teams can be created by grouping through the same energy (same colours), with students learning together towards the same task. Alternatively, or after, one child from each different colour could team up and bring their knowledge to the table to work towards the same goal. This would result in the learners sharing their different approaches to make more sense of the topic being studied. Pitching what they know to the other group could also be part of the exercise. Since they will need the four colours to really make sense of the topic, students will need each other to fully understand, but their good communication skills will also be essential to complete the learning.

I have been highly inspired by this approach, created by Brigitte Boussuat, successfully used within companies and schools of management mostly. I have used this pedagogical approach in a number of diverse schools in Europe (public and private) and discovered that learners can communicate with peers, as well as learn independently thanks to this approach. The 4Colors® compass is the educational representation of

---

32   4Colors was created by Brigitte Boussuat.

Jung[33] and Marston's[34] work on human behaviour. Like a real compass, this allows you to navigate the world of communication and identify the colour of the person you are speaking with at a certain time. Each individual is a unique blend of four different behavioural colours, represented by 4Colors® for a more intuitive understanding. Educators can definitely use this tool to communicate with peers and parents. Imagine a parent entering your classroom with a need for precision (blue energy), or speaking fast and going straight to the point (the red energy), being enthusiastic and looking for connection (the yellow energy), or a very calm parent (the green energy). If you could have a lens or compass to connect to the parent according to the energy they are giving off at that moment in time, wouldn't it be easier? This compass allows educators, parents, and children to communicate and learn efficiently together. The colours interact with each other and the blend of each of them will reflect different ways you may approach relationships to learning and others.

When the person is in the northern part of the compass, they are looking for results (blue and red colours), in the southern part, looking for a good relationship (yellow and green). When the person is in the eastern part of the compass, they need action (yellow and red) and in the western part (blue and green) they need to reflect. The red energy moves forward fast, the blue moves forward with structure and details, the green needs some time to think, and the yellow, some time to exchange. The red and yellow colours are outgoing, while the blue and

---

[33] Carl Gustav Jung, a Swiss psychiatrist who founded analytical psychology.

[34] William Moulton Marston, lawyer, inventor, and psychologist who created the DISC model for emotions and behaviour.

4: A Common Language

green colours are more introverted. Imagine if you could have a pair of colourful glasses that would show you the world through four different colourful lenses? During a training session with Brigitte Boussuat, we told a story through those different colours and only at that time did I realise how my momentary "yellowness" could annoy my colleagues who were not in this colour at the time. I realized I wanted to bring some lightness to the game when all they wanted was more structure.

When I first used the approach in class as a metacognitive and communicative tool, I was replacing a secondary French teacher for a term. I didn't know the students and they didn't know me. I decided to exchange with the students and present the *colour code*: what it meant in terms of communication as well as learning preferences. At the beginning of each session, and for over a month, I would display my colour code through post-it notes to make it clear to the learners what type of communication, as well as learning behaviour, they needed during that moment in time. When we were in the blue, we needed structure, precision, and time to go into details; in the green, more empathetic feedback and patience to work on exercises to enable learners to make links between the different exercises. In the red, we would need a more direct and faster objective to push towards challenges, and the yellow, enthusiastic and creative communication with warm rapport. We practiced this through role play and stories to tell in the different communicative approaches.

I was also extremely careful about the differences in energy between morning time and after lunch time. I would make sure to start slowly in the morning and bring energy up after lunch. When the energy level is low like after lunch, you can choose some red colour activities and little by little go to the yellow colour, then the blue and the green when energy level goes higher. Reflecting (green colour) needs energy so reading after lunch may put to sleep a whole class! One day, I even asked secondary students to show me a graph of their energy during the day. It was interesting to share mine and theirs because there were similarities and differences. Almost all of the students had more energy at the end of the day or in the evening.

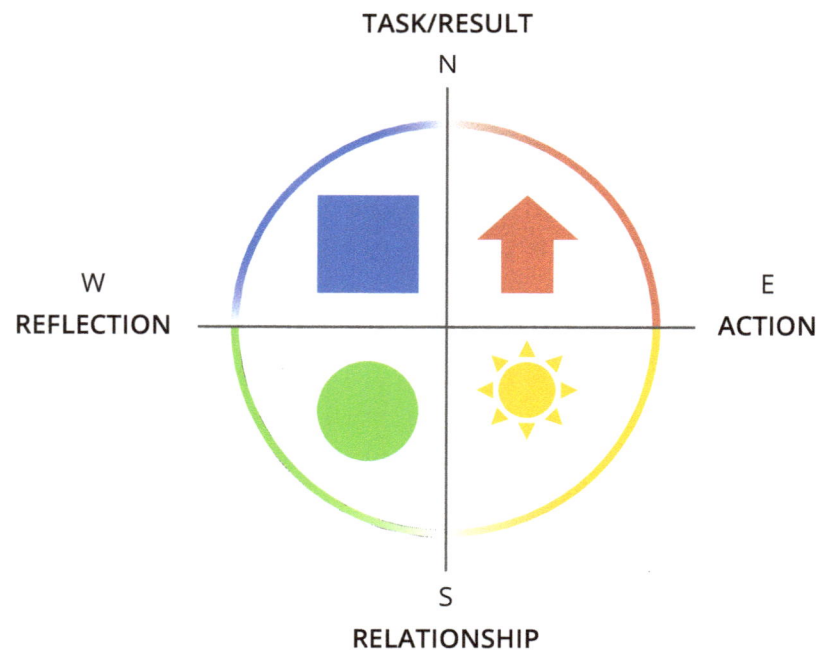

In addition, if you want to have a more engaged space, you can also use the 4Color® system through personalised spaces in the classroom or group spaces, as well as bring this colour system home or online through virtual rooms. As an example and another way to bring colours in the classroom, Marie Legrand would display the learning in her classroom as follows: the blue space would need learning material at hand and a very quiet area, the green would need learners to take time to observe and check their answers, the red would need timers to compete and explore learning, and the yellow would need to have some space and some varied and rich material to create.

We all have this mix of colours evolving in us at all times and should understand that one needs more focus than the others when learning. All throughout the day, to fully learn, we need to be aware of how all those colours are *moving*. On any given day, to fully and effectively learn, we need all four colours. After becoming aware of them, the learner can then choose to learn in red and explore, or in blue to integrate a learning sequence, in green to follow-up processes (reflect), and exchange in yellow. The emotion through colours is also expressed for self-regulation purposes at any stage of the learning: in blue with the need to step back, green to let go, the red to postpone, and yellow to enjoy. You could have some colourful cardboards for self-regulation. At a *Learning How to Learn* training, I remember a teacher in the French school in Luxembourg telling me that she would imagine her learners in colours during each session. That way, she could be more aware of what her students would need; some would need more reflection and others more action.

At first, the educator will facilitate this process by clearly stating the colour the children are being taught in. A signposted pedagogy is also an approach that could improve outputs and visible learning[35] processes. When the learning becomes more independent, the pedagogical approach would be to evolve in the learning environment you feel is more appropriate at that moment in time, and connect with others who may have the same energy in order to differentiate the learning. It is a model that fosters independence, interdependence, self-decision-making, organizational skills, responsibility, and intrinsic motivation rather than a structured factory. It is an ecological ecosystem of learners that brings the children to the centre of learning and empowers them.

To bring a *Learning How to Learn* process to the centre of learning, you would need a mindful experiential model, which can be created through five steps. Through experiences and dialogues, learners discover how these steps work in their mind to craft their own way of learning and, furthermore, allow self-esteem to kick in. It is a lot like a juice extractor — you extract what is known from the head: the juicy part of the mind! We would always start with a projection before going into the four other steps: what did I accomplish yesterday? What will I do today? How will I do it? What are the obstacles impeding my progress?

Sharing knowledge is mainly done through a mindful questioning approach to move through a more transformative and co-creative learning quest. We might say, "This is how I learnt, this is how I was

---

[35] John Hattie, director of the Melbourne Educational Research Institute, popularized the concept of visible learning.

taught, how I like learning, how I teach... so *why* don't learners understand what I am teaching them?" We need to go past this "I" and move forward, towards true active listening, to discover the other person's learning preferences. It is common for learners to be confronted with "not understanding" when a communication is relayed in a form that is not their own. It is crucial that learners recognize that when they don't understand it is not because of their inabilities.

Besides, children should be given opportunities to ask questions, explore their personal mind processes, and see that when information takes the form they personally require, they can connect to the content. The mistaken belief that understanding engages some innate or lack of ability that we possess will surely stop a lifelong learning journey from occurring. On the one hand, a mindful and agile environment will bring adaptation to new ideas, and on the other hand, communication will enable the process to create some added value.

We also need to be aware of each role within the ecosystem to adapt and be congruent with ourselves. Educators teach and facilitate content while parents support children, and both can create learning experiences that will bring enjoyment. We need to all have learning roles and embrace uncertainty when questions and answers arise. We need to learn mindfully to bring insights and dare to experiment through a cycle: exploring, following-up, and integrating, exchanging through mindful and agile learning. Interactions are spontaneous dynamics that can be engaging, supported, and facilitated but they can't be forced. To facilitate learning, we need to design content and contexts in which knowledge can be engaging.

TIME TO WONDER

How will you design content and contexts that engage learning?

How does it matter to your learners?

What if learners could engage peacefully with new habits and through what they are good at?

Mindful

Recall the quote from Albert Einstein, "Everybody is a genius. But if you judge a fish by its ability to climb a tree, it will live its whole life believing that it is stupid." Being mindful that learners do not start at the same level is not judging a fish by its ability to climb a tree, but to take each child into account! Everybody has potential but if they try to throw fish into trees and pretend they can climb, they will ignore their ability to swim and will be starved of their native element. Helping children find their strengths is not about creating diagnostics of what they don't do well but creating bridges to improvement and applied effort. If the child is often told that they forget to complete the steps in a math problem, they may eventually think they are not good at math and stop learning. What if we could show them how well they can make logical links and then ask them how they could use this to complete the steps? This strategy would bring enthusiasm and positive energy to the child.

I remember a child who told me that he couldn't learn grammar because he didn't see the use of it. When I dialogued with him, he told me that he loved building small-scale planes and would spend hours doing it. When he told me precisely what he would do to build his planes, I asked him what the model plane instruction guide had in common with grammar. He told me that grammar was a bit like a guide that could help him put words together into a sentence. He was a very communicative 16-year-old and loved expressing his thoughts. We created a few sentences together and he showed me where he could find the grammar behind it, just like the guide to build his planes. He told me that he had never thought of making this link and that he would give it a go in the future.

Moving children through their zone of proximal development[36] with some mindful support is finding a condition that activates and sustains behaviour towards a goal, and a different one for each child. It is a way for educators to think about how to push learners out of the zone they are comfortable in but not really learning anything, and into a zone that is beyond them where new learning can occur. This zone of proximal development is a metaphor. It is linking learning and development: what the young learner can do and what they can't do. It is a moving target and as a learner gains new skills and abilities, this zone moves progressively forward. If we set the learning task too far ahead and do not support them, they enter the panic zone and they cannot engage with the learning, similar to taking off the training wheels of a young child's bike too early. Learning must aim for the zone of proximal development and, when supported by someone who is more knowledgeable, learning can have a variety of internal processes. In the Montessori world, you can find guides and referees in the classroom to move the young learner into the zone of proximal development. As an educator, you can start with an easy task and move up the difficulty slowly to increase motivation.

According to Deci, Ryan,[37] and Viau,[38] if learners perceive that the activity has some value to them, if they feel competent, or if they are in control, they will be motivated. Motivation is the reason for learners'

---

36   The concept of the zone of proximal development was developed by Soviet psychologist, Lev Vygotsky.

37   The self-determination theory grew out of the work of Eduard L. Deci, American professor in psychology and M. Ryan, professor at the Institute for Positive Psychology.

38   Rolland Viau, a Canadian professor and researcher.

actions, willingness, and goals. According to Viau, motivation has its roots in the relationship between learners' perceptions and forming context. The perception of feeling competent is close to the concept of self-efficacy (believing in yourself) from Albert Bandura. If learners have high self-efficacy, they will exert sufficient effort (if done well), which can lead to successful outcomes.

If children feel competent ("I know how to do it and I am good at it"), autonomous ("I need to feel that I am at the origin of my actions"), valued for the activity ("what I do is useful"), and have social belonging ("I need to feel connected and supported by other people"), learners will make the choice of committing to achieve their goal. If one of the perceptions is negative, the most likely outcome is that the individual doesn't engage in pursuing the activity. When the choice is made, cognitive engagement and perseverance are required for obtaining achievement. The child can feel competent with a growth mindset attitude, and become autonomous if given choices as to what to learn or how to learn it, and by creating a space to exchange and connect to develop this sense of social belonging.

For me, the three important keys that keep up the learning in the classroom are a combination of an agile system, mindful thinking, and positive emotional energy that brings curiosity. Positive emotional energy can be about encouraging learners versus complimenting them. Encouraging will bring real and long-lasting respect, self-esteem, and motivation. Encouragement helps learners develop courage to grow and develop into who they want to be: capable, resilient, happy. If they feel free to make mistakes, they can learn from them and as

Rudolf Dreikurs said, "They will have the courage to be imperfect."[39] It is therefore encouraging the effort, not the learner: "You look so proud of yourself, you really proved you can do it!" rather than "I am so proud of you." Students will feel this sense of encouragement when you make comments such as: "You didn't give up even when it was hard!" instead of simply saying "Good job!" or "What a smart kid you are." Being specific and focusing on action helps the student as well: "I appreciate the way you have organised your backpack," instead of "You are so organised."

Encouraging self-reliance or enabling the learner to handle the problems required of them in life is essential. What comes with self-reliance is deep confidence in one's own abilities, the knowledge that one can rely on an unchanging part of one's self, and that one's success or emotional stability isn't reliant on the whims of others.

Then, within a clear learning system, you can understand your behavioural self and have a learning self-awareness of what the mind tells you. Thereby, starting the learning journey through a mindful and creative how-to-learn process enables children to *explore, exchange, follow-up,* and *integrate* the learning material more clearly. It is about bringing *knowledge into action*. Engaging in learning can then be a clear system that enables an agile learning approach to occur at school and at home. Agility refers here to the ability to adapt to a new learning environment, whether at home or at school: looking out for new experiences to learn from, thriving on complex challenges, and making sense of different experiences.

---

39   Rudolf Dreikurs, an Austrian psychiatrist and educator.

4: A Common Language

As I said earlier, we are interconnected learners so we can either embrace it or keep going as-is. To interact, we need to model social and emotional skills within a sustainable learning environment. The action is in the mind as well as through collaborative dialogue. It creates an active learning process that brings the learner to the centre.

 # TIME TO WONDER

What about you, what brings your motivation up and down?

What is the hesitation about getting started?

How much of your work is challenging?

What do you fear most? What makes you feel valued?

5 Facilitating Learning

Facilitating learning takes place when learners are encouraged to take more control over their own learning process. Through neuropedagogical and behavioural language, we can match the learner's energy and channel a positive and soothing outcome at home, at school, and online. For me, the key component at the heart of the "agility of mind" concept is a sunflower.

Not only is the sunflower one of the most animated, optimistic, and cheerful flowers, but the young sunflower follows every movement of the sun for better growth. So, if we want learners to rise and mature, let's get some *sun* from everyone in the ecosystem! Let's exchange at a deeper level to reveal how to share knowledge and engage.

Historically, the role of teaching has been primarily seen as delivering information to students in order for them to gain a foundational knowledge of many subjects, and score appropriately on tests and standardized assessments. Redefining educators' purpose and function in the classroom is critical in order to ensure student success and relevance in the 21st century.

Learning and teaching innovation has been rooted in various educational philosophies, for instance, Reggio Emilia, Montessori, Waldorf, Summerhill, applied Buddhism, and many more. Despite different practices, these philosophies share a focal point: a humanistic approach with a learner-oriented and diversified education. By spelling out their own philosophies as concrete actions, these teaching approaches combine subjects into a set of integrated packages. Most alternative schools also tend to set up learning outdoors, working as a team, facilitating learning, tutoring, and teaching in classrooms together. Elizabeth Gonzales, an enthusiastic and innovative positive educator, has introduced me to an online personalised lifelong learning system called *Learning One to One,* which has a facilitating approach to learning, a framework that enables each learner to practice at their own pace. Erika Twani, the CEO of Relational Learning says: "The right use of AI develops students' agency, personalizes students' learning process rather than content, and has the ultimate goal of developing competencies and habits of the mind."[40] Using technology and interactions together to realize individual potential is the future of learning.

The traditional concept of schooling, based on knowledge acquisition where there is one classroom, one teacher, one class, and one subject at a time is being increasingly questioned. Since it will be this way for a while, educators need to rethink the interaction between practices and education. Cognition can't be developed without social and emotional practices, especially with technology evolving so quickly. Learning is becoming increasingly blended or hybrid, which means that face-to-face or peer-to-peer learning will be combined with virtual learning environments. Educators' strategic guidance is crucial and facilitating learning through learners' strengths will be indispensable in the roles of educators.

When I think of facilitating learning, I like to share the metaphor of the nose cone of a rocket: the educator leader has the guidance system that controls the flight direction of the rocket. By adding weight to the nose (power), the rocket stabilizes and goes higher when it has sufficient thrust. Therefore, co-creating a sense of direction is the thrust, which educators can give to children. They are given power (the weight of the rocket) to choose their direction only when we believe in them and search for the best way to move forward. Educators will then facilitate the children's learning "take off" and turn them into learning leaders who will find their own power. Dr Mihaly Csikszentmihalyi, author of Flow: *The Psychology of Optimal Experience,* relates to authentic classrooms

---

[40] Learn more about Erika Twani on the Microsoft Alumni Network page at https://www.microsoftalumni.com/s/1769/19/interior aspx?sid=1769&gid=2&pgid=2435

that are in the flow, and Daniel Goleman, the author of *Emotional Intelligence: Why It Can Matter More Than IQ*, would "foresee a day when education will routinely include essential human competencies such as self-awareness, self-control, and empathy, as well the art of listening."

POWER (can + will) + ENERGY + FLOW

=

PERSONAL LEARNING ENGAGEMENT

 # TIME TO WONDER

How is your energy used?

How is it wasted?

On a scale from 1 to 10, how much power are you giving to the learners?

How much energy are learners giving to their learning?

Even if we often start learning as a solo process, most learning is the result of an interaction between learners, either through time via written communication, or through space via oral communication. Language allows us to organize our thoughts and share our ideas. At the beginning of the 20th century, in cognitive psychology, Gregory Bateson brought the communication theory to the forefront, as well as methods of innovation; in the 70s, Richard Bandler and John Grinder developed their neurolinguistic programming ideas. Those models allow us to understand and master our communication skills. This approach will be presented in the second part of the book.

According to Antoine de la Garanderie, learning is a behaviour as well as a mental introspective process. He wrote that in order to facilitate knowledge positively, we must understand that:

- The learner must be responsible: they need to choose to be challenged and accept to explore or not, by being empowered. We can ask questions or expect a learner to learn but we can't force them to answer or to learn.

- Every learner can learn: everyone has their own resources to learn and there is no innate gift, but much more the idea that the brain is plastic. So many children believe that they have special abilities, and for that reason decide not to try learning a subject.

- A learner is someone different from us; there are as many learners as there are human beings so we need to accept diversity. We tend to think that if we have some similarities in tastes, we will learn the same way. As educators, we need to be reminded how each brain in the class learns differently than us.

- The learning process needs to be positive: since failure is not accepted as a fatality, knowledge is built on successful domains. If the child loves to cook, we will ask them how they do it. We need to strengthen what the learner is good at instead of fixing them.

We often forget that learners are leaders of their own learning and that the ideal leader seeks to create an environment where there is free flow of thought and high levels of understanding. The Broaden and Build theory, developed by Professor Barbara Fredrickson in 1998, says that positive emotions do much more than cause us happiness in the moment, they also broaden behaviours she called thought-action repertoires, such as awareness, discovery, and curiosity. The more positive emotions we experience, the more flexible and creative we are. The perceptions of emotion are not universal so naming them can be useful when the learning stops.

"Quiet Leadership," described by David Rock[41] helps improve on the thinking and brings transformation, as well as improving performance at work. I believe this can also be useful at school and at home. This 6-step approach brings a desire to help individuals grow through a

---

41 Dr. David Rock is the director of the Neuroleadership Institute, a global initiative bringing neuroscientists and leadership experts together to build a new science for leadership development.

sustained leadership style: empathetic, self-aware, and challenging.

David Rock is very thorough in explaining the six steps and there is a lot you can learn when working with them. In short, here they are:

1. *Think about thinking*: keep focussed on strengths and solutions, challenge the thinking.

2. *Listen for potential*: enable self-learning and growth.

3. *Speak with intent:* succinct, specific, and generous.

4. *Dance towards insight:* awareness of dilemma, reflection, "aha" moments, and motivation.

5. *Create new thinking:* current reality, explore alternatives, tap their energy.

6. *Follow up:* feeling model (facts, emotions, encourage, learning, implications, and new goal).

What does it look like when interactive learning has stopped?

Imagine a learner called Julie using her calculator incorrectly and another learner, Sarah, offering her some advice and then returning to her exercise. But later, Sarah notices that Julie is still misusing it and decides to sit with her until she gets it right. Over the next few days, Sarah notices that Julie is defensive when she offers her feedback, and avoids talking to her. Sarah is really puzzled because all she wants is to help Julie, and she can't figure out why she is reacting so badly to her support. If Sarah had known about the following scarf model, she would have understood that Julie felt threatened by her actions.

To collaborate efficiently with others when facilitating learning, David Rock also presents an effective tool that influences our behaviour in social situations and can be an added value to the 4Colors® communicative approach. This model, called SCARF, was developed in 2008 stands for five key domains:

1. *Status*: our relative importance to others (How am I compared to...?)

2. *Certainty*: our ability to predict the future (How certain am I?)

3. *Autonomy*: our sense of control over events (Can I make a choice?)

4. *Relatedness*: how safe we feel with others (How connected am I? Am I "in" or "out"?)

5. *Fairness*: how just we perceive the exchanges between people to be (Is this fair?)

This model is based on the neuroscience research that suggests that these five social domains trigger the same threat and reward responses in our brain that enable us to survive. For example, learners might perceive being left out of an activity as a threat to their status and relatedness; research shows that the brain can send out a 'danger' signal in response to this stimulation. Moreover, when we feel threatened either physically or socially, the release of cortisol (the stress hormone) affects our creativity and productivity. We literally can't think straight, thus increasing the feeling of being threatened. We then can't learn any more.

When I think of facilitating learning, I think of the SCARF model and the following quadrant. I think of the learners I might have in my sessions, and Alice from Lewis Carroll's *Alice in Wonderland* comes to mind. There is one lesson in the novel that we can all reflect on, which is about growing, taking risks, challenging ourselves, and being curious when learning: crawling down a rabbit hole might be a big risk, but Alice decides to follow the white rabbit, resulting in a magical journey. It is not all smooth but by the time she wakes up from Wonderland she's armed with new experiences to help her navigate real life.

How many "Alice" learners do you have in your classroom: fully immersed in the experience?

How many "Hesitant Caterpillar" learners do you have: reserved about opening up to the experience?

What about the "Disengaged Dormouse" learners: emotionally disengaged in the process?

Or maybe "White Rabbit" learners who need to go fast, straight to the point?

5: Facilitating Learning

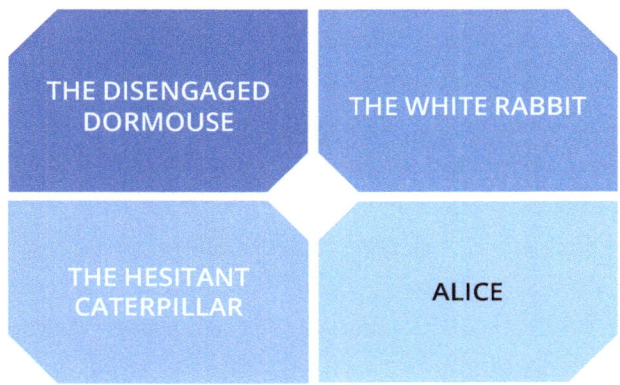

Where do you think your learner leaders are in this quadrant?

You can show this quadrant to the learners and ask them to share with you some more personal characteristics for each role that is laid out. They might share what makes them immerse themselves in the learning experience, what makes them hesitant, what disengages them, and when they need to go straight to the point. I once asked the students and they told me that they were more likely to immerse themselves when they chose what to do. Additionally, they are hesitant to learn when they don't know the subject, disengage when they don't like the subject, and want to get straight to the point when they already know the topic or when they are tired. One went so far as to say, "I always want to go straight to the point, otherwise I fall asleep!"

Then, once an understanding of each role has been established, ask them where they feel they are at the moment in time. Again, moving from one spot to another one is up to the learners because you can't force anything to happen. You can encourage them to reflect on what they do to move from Hesitant Caterpillar to Alice. You can show them they can choose which role they want to fit in and therefore find their own process to learn. It is about the *how* and not the outcome at this moment in time. It is not about doing your best but instead the focus can be on how everyone can do better. These questions give learners the opportunity to ask themselves, to choose to explore, and give it a try.

How can we move the learner to a more positive emotional state?

To eliminate threats and maximize reward you should check what each learner needs most at any given time:

- **Status**
  Give feedforward (positive feedback) and praise effort regularly.

- **Certainty**
  Break down complex tasks into smaller chunks to develop flexibility and resilience.

  Give a sense of learning direction to show them that they are on the right track.

- **Autonomy**
  Co-create processes and show trust by including them in the decision-making process.
  Encourage more initiative.

- **Relatedness**
  Create buddy systems or mentoring arrangements and check

regularly how they are doing by organizing special one-to-one sessions.

- **Fairness**
  Be open and honest about what's going on and why. Encourage mutual acceptance and never show favour or exclude people on purpose. Clarify goals and roles and get learners' input.

You might be thinking that bringing all the necessary steps to a learning session may be difficult, but by using the coloured compass, being clear about the process, and creating a buddy system, I can reassure you that this approach moves learners to a positive emotional space that will engage them. The SCARF model brings more awareness to the process.

A Whisperer as Facilitator

Educators may now be facing one of the biggest challenges to date: the success of learning is global and it depends on the educators to change it, and to evolve with it. What can be done? Continuing traditional roles of the *sage on the stage* will be unfavourable for the learners, so what about making small shifts in how we create experiences in classrooms and online, to become facilitators, guides, and mentors of the learners' journey?

Imagine yourself standing in a natural environment, surrounded by starlings, flying around you. As they fly, every starling seems to be connected to the others when switching directions, swooping high and low, and creating beautiful formations in the sky. If you watch closely, you can see that there is no single bird controlling the way in which all the birds fly. You may simply observe that one takes the lead and each and every other bird follows, as if there was some kind of whispering in the sky. There is a *quiet leader*[42] in each of them. If we could reproduce this dance it would encourage certain interactions that are designed with the learner and would facilitate learning. When facilitating, the way to human connection is to all share the same goal, a common vision, and a way to feel stronger together. Sincerity, empathy, synchronicity, and engagement enable this dance to happen.

Synchronicity is a concept developed by psychologist Carl Jung. It describes a perceived meaningful coincidence, or, in Jung's words, an "acausal connecting principle"[43] in which external events might align with an individual's experience, perhaps mirroring or echoing their personal worries or beliefs. By modelling the right behaviours, like enthusiasm or empathy in the classroom, you can orchestrate synchronicity through colourful *learning capsules* throughout the day. You can frame some after lunch with brain gyms to bring the energy up or yellow capsules to exchange. Even distance learning can allow synchronicity, using the same agility of mind approach to learning. Communicating through the 4Colors® approach can also bring synchronicity in the learning sessions.

"When we trust, we feel better and more positive," says Judith E. Glaser. "When we experience high levels of trust, we feel empowered to work out issues and challenges, open ourselves to new experiences, and link with others in a way that is sometimes called synchronicity."[44]

---

[42] David Rock, author of the book *Quiet Leadership: Six Steps to Transforming Performance at Work*

[43] Jung, Carl Gustav. *Synchronicity*. Princeton University Press, 2012.

[44] Judith E. Glaser (personal communication, 2016)

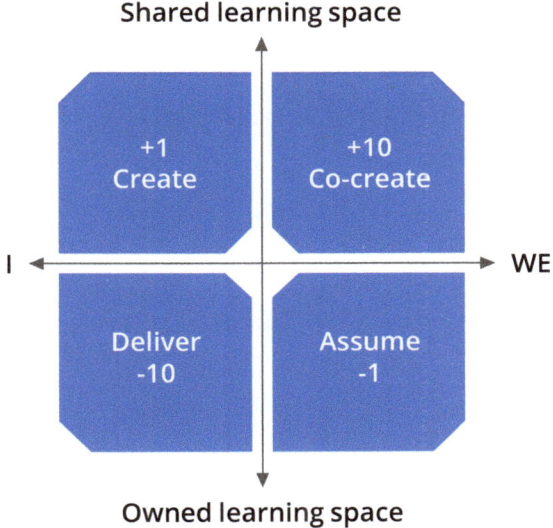

When facilitating learning, we first create tasks that need to be completed beforehand in order to invite learners to participate, contribute, and co-create. The tasks can be done through a clear iterative approach on exploring, following up, exchanging, and integrating (through problem/quest solving, application, or restitution). These tasks have essential prior knowledge learnt through pre-learning online experiences, as well as post-learning ones. It is in this agile and structured space that interactions can be brought. Secondly, we need to bring both astonishment and interactions in learning contexts to create engagement. Thirdly, we need to accept mistakes as a lifelong learning journey to reveal character strengths and invite learners to engage with imperfection and vulnerability. Facilitating is creating learning contexts that are incomplete and astonishing. We need to shift from imposing our knowledge expertise to facilitate learning for a lifelong learning journey, for a more engaged and collaborative process. There is nothing about undermining our expertise, but only changing our role and behaviour, and being clear about this role in order for a different learning process to happen.

Where are you in your facilitating role?

What would it take for you to feel more engaged or want to co-create with learners?

Ecology of Mind[45]

Learning never stops so let's learn from one another and push the act of *questioning*. One of the key practices of facilitating is asking questions, instead of bringing content or rushing to give answers to learners. It is our responsibility to refrain from sharing our ideas for solutions and instead invite the input of all concerned parties to bring a collective piece of intelligence to uncover possible answers. The aim is to facilitate learners' interactions. As a parent or educator, we wish to bring content and answers. However, what if we could pause to observe how learners learn? I am fascinated by the way learners become attentive, understand, memorize, reflect, or create, how they use content, move with it, and interact with it. It would be a shift of focus to lead to learners' transformation rather than test results: a self-awareness, a space for listening and connecting.

Awareness in the classroom can be created through presenting clear

---

[45] Gregory Bateson, *Steps to an Ecology of Mind*. Learn more at: http://www.naturearteducation.org/AnEcologyOfMind.htm

objectives on the educator's part (orally expressed as well as written) and some sharing about the learners' goals. You can also involve your students by asking them if they prefer an activity at home, in class, together, individually, in writing, or through conversation with a partner. Linking your class learning to the real world can help the students see the relevance of what they learn. Usually learners learn because "My teacher told me to," or "It is necessary for the exam." Show them how they can learn the content more efficiently and have fun with it. Give them some choice with multiple options in colours and ask them to try out a different colour each time. It is all about mediating the learning and not exercising authority.

To create some trustful and engaging learning environments, allow group and one-on-one discussions (yellow or green space), as well as calling on one another for help, rather than going directly to the educator. Create some curious spaces by asking questions that don't have one answer. You can also create some guests' spaces and collaborate with educators to teach related lessons in different subjects (like it is done in the International Baccalaureate program). Through this interactive method, have learners explain what they learn to someone who doesn't know the material. In Finland, instead of asking the teachers to teach the lesson for other children, the responsibility is given to the pupils; it is called "The Finnish Double Flip." Younger children can actually teach older children. Role play different scenarios, create quests in colours, or play games to illustrate lessons.

When connecting, the educator should give context for each lesson, showing how it relates to things that the learners might be experiencing. As an example, children can start by creating an "avatar" in colour to begin their learning quest and create their *dream team*. How much of each colour would they need? Would they need more or less action, exchanges, reflection, and results-oriented moments? You can give them some coloured sticky dots to create this avatar and let their imagination flow. You can ask each of them to imagine what strengths their own avatar will be displaying in the learning project. Starting through imagination is one of the essential ingredients for engagement.

The educator can also tie the material to other lessons, classes, subjects, current events, or real-life examples. Understanding why the lesson is relevant to the students' lives, and why it should matter to them is important. You can also share some anecdotes about your own life. I remember, when teaching French, my 15-year-old students at the International Australian School of Singapore asking me to share some of my stories from growing up in France. They loved it so much that I started to link some personal stories to my lessons. During this same class, as I was teaching the topic of weather, I skyped with a French person and asked the students to prepare and ask some questions about the weather. The students told me they loved it because it was real and concrete for them. It was also unexpected, so they were really surprised, which further helped cement the learning in their minds. It was unexpected for me too, since I decided to redesign the session at the last minute!

Learners can find various resources but at times it is hard for them to know if the information can be trusted, so this example is one possible facilitation to help alleviate that issue. Creating some experiences through facilitation is something they won't find online, but it is something that will empower them. They go from consumers to actors, being at the centre of learning. Educators are constantly competing with the engaging experiences that children have online. The educator turns from being a planner to a producer. Like a producer, the educator is practical and creative. They are both the driving force right through to the end, and are the overall decision makers. They come up with story ideas, they spot and solve potential difficulties, delegate certain responsibilities, create a good working environment, and constantly communicate with everyone to make everything run smoothly. Engagement is the measure (how you involve learners with the content) and motivation the driver (a need that drives the learning). To be engaged, children need to care about the activities they will be doing, be responsible, and contribute to the learning community. So, let's mediate the way.

The key to learning is the ability of *learning to learn*. For Gregory Bateson, anything else is just static and finished, because it doesn't evolve. Plutarch wrote, "Education is the kindling of a flame, not the filling of a vessel."[46] Those words are as true today as they were two thousand years ago. The vessel-filling activity remains today in the education system. So, if the kindling of the flame is the ultimate core of all profound learning, why don't we move towards finding the kindling that will light up the learners' minds? We need to find a way, a space, where quality interactions can be triggered. For that, we need to think of what matters to the learners, and what would be an added value for them.

---

46   1992, Essays by Plutarch, Translation by Robin Waterfield, On Listening, Quote Page 50, Penguin Classics, London and New York.

TIME TO WONDER

What is the pattern that connects the content you teach?

What is the importance of that content to the learners?

Fertility of Time

The educators' challenge when teaching is a set curriculum and testing that they have to race through as fast as possible. But we know that learning takes time, practice and requires patience and effort. Engaging a child in their learning journey at home and at school can take time. It is like cultivating a cherry tree to grow cherries: most cherry trees do not bear fruit for the first year or two of their lives. Some cherry trees take as long as four years to bear their first fruit. By giving the best autonomous environment possible and a nurturing communicative approach through the creation of a co-learning space, acquired with patience, you will be growing some cherries. Like the gardener, both educators and parents are in charge of encouraging growth. Over time, energy and power will be released from the child and growth will happen. Let's observe, dialogue, listen, praise, and adapt projects together!

By focusing on creating micro-learning sessions through questioning and colours, we will design a sustainable facilitating model and foster positive interactions. It could appear time-consuming but when it is done through a clear learning model, more material can be covered. Spaced repetition[47] is a more effective technique for learning because it is in synchronicity with the manner our brains function, and time studying information you already know is not wasted. Micro learnings that are spaced out are keys to long-lasting information. Researchers have proven that the brain is not well-adapted to storing lots of new information in short periods of time. The psychologist Hermann

---

47 Professor C. A. Mace proposed the spaced repetition notion in his book, *The Psychology of Study*.

Ebbinghaus[48] discovered in 1885 that people forget 80% of newly learned material within 24 hours. His research on the capabilities of human memory led to the so-called *forgetting curve*. That is why learning techniques like cramming are unsuccessful for long-term benefits.

We can also enable learning transfer to happen by creating insights for a lifelong learning quest, and by encouraging us to think about our own thinking. What researchers[49] explain about transfer is that knowledge needs to start with a precise context, then build through similar situations (not the same ones) in an explicit way. Then, little by little, learners will decontextualize knowledge themselves through a metacognitive approach. Only then this abstract structure can be re-contextualized by the learners. How could we create learning environments that are sustainable?

We need to think of the pre-learning and the post-learning projects and how the learning can be sustained in the long run. We also need to think about children's own life-long learning quest for a positive approach to learning. Not only does it enable the learner to be joyful but it also produces positive added value for children. What will be the added value for the child? What outcomes do we want to create? Then, the learners need to be agile and resilient in the changes they face. This is seen as creating sustainable quality time since learning needs time and energy. We need to consider the consequences in the short term

---

48 Hermann Ebbinghaus, a German psychologist who pioneered the experimental study of memory and is known for his discovery of the forgetting curve and spacing effect.

49 Philippe Meirieu, French researcher and writer, specialist in the science of education and pedagogy.

and create learning in a way that stands the test of time. What if what we learnt did not *lose* value over time but instead *gained* value?

Whatever we create, we need to remain agile and able to adapt to changing circumstances. What if learners were the *source connectors* to be built into the learning creation? Finally, to move forward, we need to anticipate future trends or the unforeseeable, as opposed to responsiveness in the learning system. We will create a proactive quality in the learning process. For that, we empower the learners to respond to a number of possible scenarios. This builds an agile system that would sustain itself.

For a sustainable learning process, we need to embrace the reality of today and build in the resilience and agility to adapt to constantly changing conditions and the concept of anticipatory thinking about the future. We should also add *quality time* for insights in the learning quest to facilitate learning processes. We need the right tools and the right energy to go on this particular quest. The result is finding the right content in a certain space and time to create flow. The way learning can emerge is in terms of balancing the right interactions in conjunction with the right energy and movement. Therefore there is a difference between delivering static content, or focusing on what it can offer, and going beyond itself.

6
Learning Experiences

An Iterative Learning

Today, transforming the learning environment is essential since it is a necessity to be able to come safely through this new era. Young learners are facing inevitable difficulties that need to be addressed. For me, interactions are the backbone of this transformation. This is the reason why we need to foster interactions in learning contexts. Interactions need to be clearly facilitated but not forced and for that, contexts need to be fertile. But how can we foster that agile, mindful learning and positive communication? What process would we engage in? How can we create a context that will be a co-creative one?

The iterative process means that the learner proceeds in their competence by several trials of acquisition and application. The first trial to acquire knowledge may be exploratory, supported by exchanges or searches on the internet. This first step brings mistakes, as learning phases and learners can take risks and gain experience. These first trials need to be repeated by similar situations in a precise context and little by little. It puts special emphasis on engaging with learning and on supporting self-directed and group learning. Prototyping a supportive environment for learning with consultations during and after face-to-face or remote experiences will be developed and evaluated.

Learning makes me think of mindful breathing. Breathing is essential to life; it allows the body to attain the energy it needs to sustain itself. If you add mindfulness to breathing, it will change your way of being in the world. If learning energy is released mindfully, learning potential can be released. It is when this living phase is present that we can start facilitating, through questioning, *in and out* reflective mind *movements* to bring some insights when the learner is ready. Then, facilitators need to keep being learners themselves and be aware that children know the way it works best for them. We need a space that brings interactions and immediate feedback to support learning: project, explore, integrate, follow up, and exchange. Creating colourful spaces brings to life learning spaces that truly foster interactions, and for that purpose, another process needs to be co-designed with the learner: an iterative one.

Learning through Experiences

In fact, this process can't be created without the learners themselves. We need to create it in a way that can be supported by learners and that encourages the right interactions. We need to work together, collaborate, and interact. The creation of knowledge can only happen in a collaborative dynamic and therefore be based on interactions. So, before a result can be created, interactions are at the heart of the process. We can therefore differentiate the subject on the understanding of how each of the children learn and keep a time frame that will be the same for everyone while still allowing everyone to go at their own pace.

The iterative process is a five-way co-creative process through a colourful quest. This is the facilitator's role: to bring it to life, little by little. Facilitating learning is like meeting someone for the first time, as are interactions with learners. Imagine that you're meeting the learner for the first time each time you meet with them and you will become a lot more curious. When we go and meet a person for the first time, our senses are sharp and we are open and curious to listen. We therefore need this space to prepare for this new encounter: a calm but joyful place is vital for the learning journey to happen. We can call this the *flow* area. According to where the child is with their own energy at that moment in time in the colour process (blue, yellow, red, or green), they will be able to quiet their mind by being aware of it. This *flow* area is a way to recharge the energy, become more aware of our strengths, and learn about our emotions and our behavioural state at the moment. It is the part when children can pause to be mindful.

In each learning phase of the journey, intention in the project needs to happen first. An engaging dialogue will enable children to choose a personal project and a direction to study. The child thinks of what they know and what they need to know and how to study. There is no right or wrong answer, just a listening and inquiry approach from facilitators. A step back is also taken alone to answer or create questions. Right after, moving forward can be done. Dialoguing implies interaction and cooperation. As soon as we cooperate, we need to adapt our energy to the other person's energy, and we need to know what intention they will be putting in. It is not about our own intention but the learners' clear intentions, which will be the first part of an engagement framework to share knowledge in a future collaborative vision. We can also think of who would be able to support learners on the learning journey. This iterative process incorporates the feedforward process whenever needed. It is through these five ways of learning that a clear context can be created and truly support the learners it is serving. It is the bulk of the creative and agile process that is being done through critical thinking skills. This second way will depend on the energy chosen: explore, integrate, follow-up, or exchange.

Let's imagine that the learner starts their iteration with *exploring*. It is learning through exploration and testing hypotheses, as well as the use of a critical thinking process. This part could also be used to test knowledge through a defined time. Theories and facts are explored and not taught. The third way could be *integrating* new knowledge by comparing differences and similarities in a context that makes sense to the learner at the beginning. The "what" and "how" can be presented by creating a post, an article, a video, a creative piece of art, some music, some photos with comments, a virtual reality quest of what has been understood. The fourth way could be the *following up,* dedicated to locating the source of knowledge (theory), thinking on the thinking process, and making links visible. This part is meant to provide time to reflect on new discoveries. The fifth way could be *exchanging*. This process needs learners' input and can be used any time in the process. This part can also be dedicated to the co-development or implementation of the learning process. In the end, this moment brings full understanding as well as knowledge transfer as the result of turning a collective and creative piece of personal work into a more abstract piece of work. All learners have their own expertise that they bring to the group, so we can also think of who can share the content knowledge between peers, and even within the ecosystem.

After understanding everyone's intention, and while following up, exploring, and integrating, the educator and peers will listen and share thoughts or knowledge to validate or invalidate. This is learning by exchanging and designing a bigger challenging framework, within the collective intelligence. In fact, depending on the learners' energy, the learners will move around this iterative process and will be able to go back and forth in the learning cycle. Each learning part dedicates support to the ever-changing needs of the learners. The following is the iterative model — choose your colour:

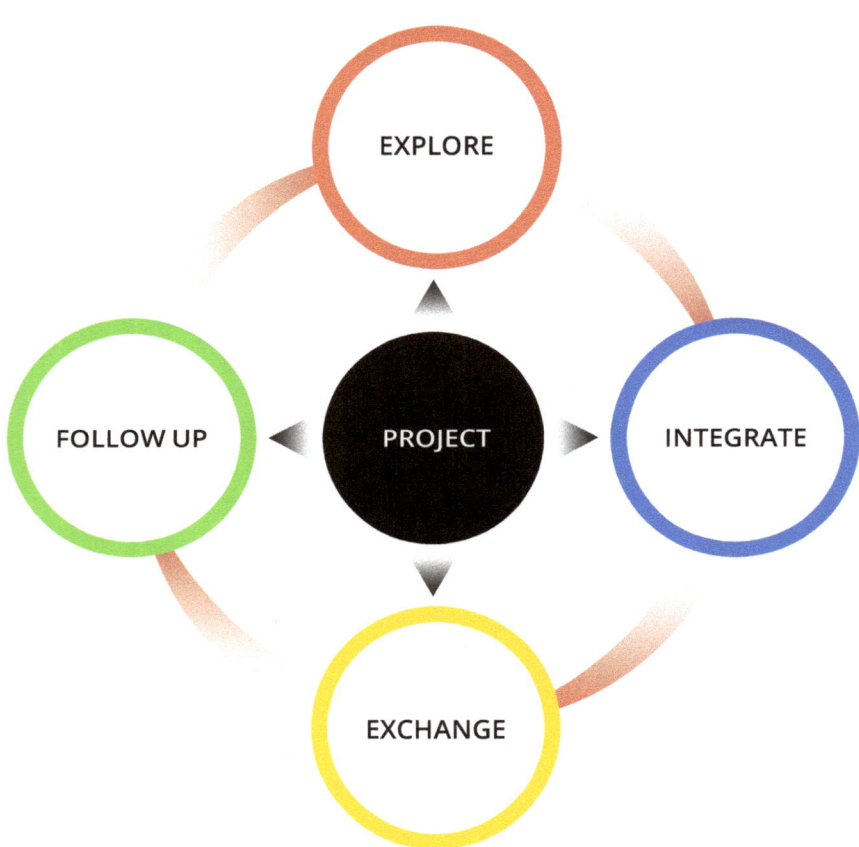

Insights

Collecting insights when learning is to believe that learning needs to be from within. I believe that learners are the experts in how they learn and that the educators' role is that of facilitators or *mediators of knowledge*. We all go towards learning in a different manner, on our own paths and most of the time unconsciously. A learner who starts by experimenting without reflecting will miss important parts of their learning. We need to actively involve every child in their own learning project to allow them to be engaged in the process. The key is to do it through a successful, collaborative process and to shift from teaching to facilitating learning. This may appear like chaos, and sometimes even feel like it, but it needs to be seen as a guiding process. We need to enable children to develop a sense of ownership of their own learning project; since they are experts on their own learning, children need to become aware of their expertise. This expertise needs to be assessed, which is how patterns emerge: insights. Those insights are then incorporated into the learning project design, through phases of developing and maturing. This process needs to be owned by the learners themselves and the translation of the "what" and "how" to learn can be translated into a learning quest.

Mindsets

This process can only work if children undergo a shift in mindset. Not only do children have to become aware that they will learn through quests, but educators will need to shift from only sharing knowledge to also facilitating knowledge. The hardest part of the beginning of this process is uncertainty, because we don't jump to solutions but instead, it is with a collective search for the right questions and possible answers that we lead the process towards. It is like figuring out a complex puzzle with many tiny pieces without having any idea of what the final overall picture of the puzzle is. Therefore, participating in the learning process with an open mind and allowing the collective intelligence to influence input and build emerging ideas is essential. This will also be difficult at times because learners might come to sessions with pre-conceived ideas and miss a chance to be enriched by the collective intelligence. We need to be comfortable with uncertainty to move forward with it.

It is essential to trust the learning process by actively participating in it and watching interactions generate added value.

A Common Project

The learning process needs to have a vision, a project, and a purpose based on reinforcing this sense of community and encouraging them to take their own responsibility and action. One of the many things we will remember during this global health crisis, the Covid-19 pandemic, is this: we saw hundreds of community tasks around specific projects being created and followed. When people were working together, they would sit down and find solutions to bring the project together because they knew why they were doing it. When tired or demotivated, they would remember why, and how important it was. This process was a circular one not a linear one: it needed to have an open process, and everyone needed to have a common *why*. It was about creating contexts through collective insights. Through this "why" and "how," there was a willingness to take risks and be motivated to try new things. It was essential to be flexible through a common project; we couldn't be defensive, but we needed to stay engaged through that common objective. We all needed to be open to new experiences together through a behavioural measure and a non-cognitive one. We could bring feedforward to improve, read, or keep up in our knowledge, take on new roles, and interact with others from different backgrounds, test things out, and evaluate with an *after-action review*. We need to learn from experience through an ongoing day-to-day common project.

TIME TO WONDER

How would you like to create experiences as opposed to content-oriented lessons?

What could be your purpose-based project?

How would you bring interactions together within the learning environment?

How would you feel about asking your learners, "what are your insights from the session?"

Part 1:
In a Nutshell

How can we reach out to children today? How can we engage children who are actually willing to learn through a combination of fun, knowledge, and technology? Why do kids need educator-leaders who can show them the way to mindful communicative and agile learning, as well as how to use the learning processes to adapt easily at school and at home?

We live in a world of rapid change where the entire educational system is constantly challenged; a world being shaped in a context and time that are different to what went on in our past; a world where lifelong learning is key to employability and where this young learning generation calls for more collaboration and co-creation. Every learner wants to succeed. Every parent dreams of seeing their children happy and living a successful life. Every educator wishes to see children thrive and does everything in their power to make it happen.

Getting to know oneself better, and becoming aware of our learning and teaching preferences, facilitates communication and thus the performance and well-being of the learners. It is on the basis of a common,[50]

---

50 On the basis of the 4Colors compass, developed by Brigitte Boussuat, which is the pedagogical representation of Jung and Marston's work.

clear, and easy language that we will focus on. By multiplying quality interactions, we will allow learners to better understand everyone's expectations and needs to share the ingredients for success. In addition, the discovery of *Learning How to Learn* pedagogical tools guarantee the richness of interactions and therefore gives everyone the means to adjust their practices.

Learning through interactions is key to helping young learners develop a successful and happy engaging learning journey:

- Interactions between cognition and emotion that bring a mindful exploration of thoughts and actions together. You will find simple tools to develop a curious learning mindset for young learners and reactivate the learning when stopped (individual mindset).

- Peer-to-peer interactions at school and online that are about iterative learning, learning strategies, and mentoring/coaching actions. You will find a compass to develop mindful and agile learning behaviour for a more engaging environment (collective behaviour).

- Interactions with others in the community at large to bridge school and home and define the right supportive learning actions. You will be able to use a model and multiple keys for your communication and bring the agile *Learning How to Learn* model to the home (community communication).

PART 2
The Agility of Mind

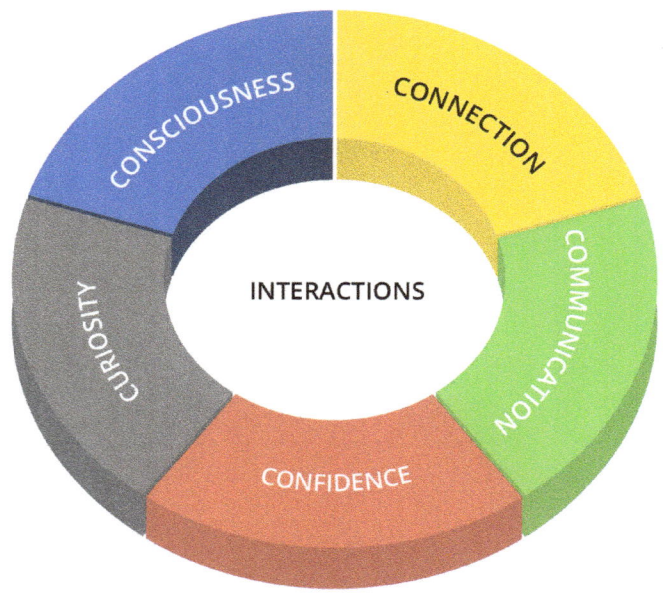

The 5 Cs

7
A Caring and Engaging Environment which Relies on Interactions

The 5 Cs

Agility of mind brings the ability to think about our thinking, our e.motion, and our behaviour to the forefront. We see change as a positive growth of experience. Expect the unexpected to change the thinking in our head, leading us to want to understand how our learning changes our reality through insightful moments. With this curious mindset, we realize the power of peer-to-peer and community interactions.

Change disturbs our predictable patterns. But if we do things that work, and it often works, we want to repeat them so we feel good about the outcome. We can feel safe and when we do, our levels of cortisol are lower and our mind is open to explore, discover, and learn without being scared to make mistakes that may damage our ego or reputation or even our confidence.

Change brings with it challenges. When we limit or minimize the fear associated with challenges or risk of failure, we are increasing our chances for success. Agility of mind gives the ability to explore, reflect, follow-up, and exchange our thinking all together and therefore change the way we navigate the challenges of learning.

Mastering the agility of mind is bringing greater awareness over both inner and outer spaces. Aligning projection and result (thinking and action) is the core of the agility of mind and practicing it can bring success. Success is something the brain likes, a reward for doing something right. The neurotransmitters associated with success are highly reinforcing learning new things and taking up challenges while feeling good about ourselves.

The brain likes certainty and it is what we do to predict the future.

7: A Caring and Engaging Environment which Relies on Interactions

And, if we are right about our hypothesis, we become more confident in taking risks even in the face of failure. By applying the agility of mind, you are giving new directions to mistakes and labelling them as experiments.

8
Consciousness

Go Forward

Before sharing knowledge, it is essential to know more about ourselves. Therefore, connecting with ourselves, our way of behaving and teaching, is essential to connect with learners. Being aware of your own sharing and learning style as well as sharing this content with learners will enable them to connect to their own way of learning.

Identify Your Teaching Preferences

According to a recent study in France, 67% of educators teach as they learn. Therefore, it can be expected that parents would also share knowledge in the same way they themselves learn.[51] John Medina[52] recommends that educators use an MBTI-type profile[53] to learn about

---

51   Survey from the National Ministry of education in France by Catherine Moisan (2013).

52   John Medina, a developmental molecular biologist, founding director of the Talaris Research Institute, and author of *Brain Rules: 12 Principles for Surviving and Thriving at Work, Home and School*, 2008.

53   The Myers Briggs Type Indicator personality inventory is an introspective self-report questionnaire indicating psychological preferences.

their own behavioural styles, but I personally would rather choose the word "habit" or "preference." As discussed previously, more useful is the 4Colors® approach, developed on the basis of the work of C.G. Jung and W.M. Marston, that makes it possible to characterize behavioural preferences, at a certain moment in time, symbolized by the four colours: red, yellow, green, and blue.

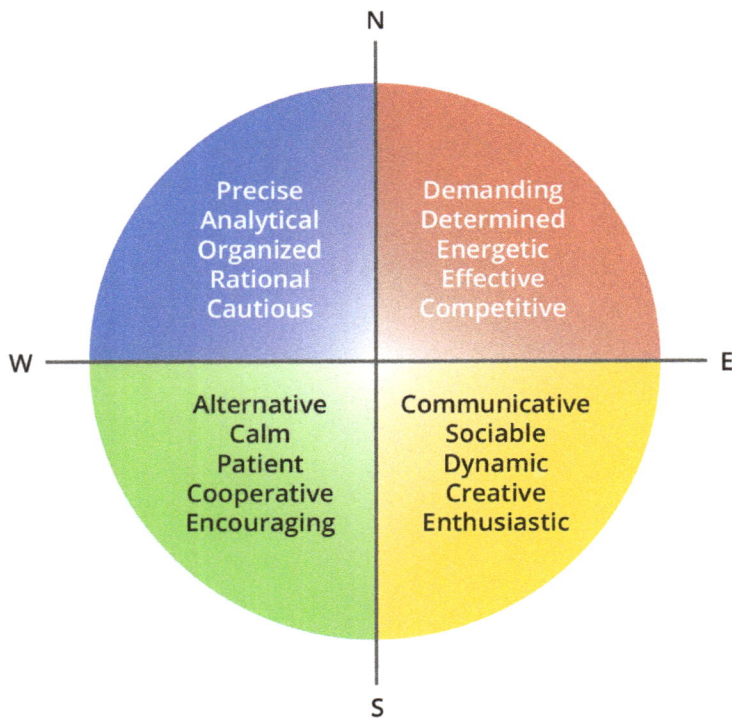

ACTION:
When you share knowledge, be aware of the colour you are in.

Identify Your Learning Preferences

Each brain is unique, and malleable. Eric Kandel, Nobel Prize winner in medicine, has shown that learning physically alters the wiring of our brain.[54] The neuroplasticity of the brain, identified as early as 1967 by Paul Bach-y-Rita, has been widely explored since the 1990s. Based on the work of C.G. Jung and the 4Colors® method, this compass allows us to identify the different needs of learners.

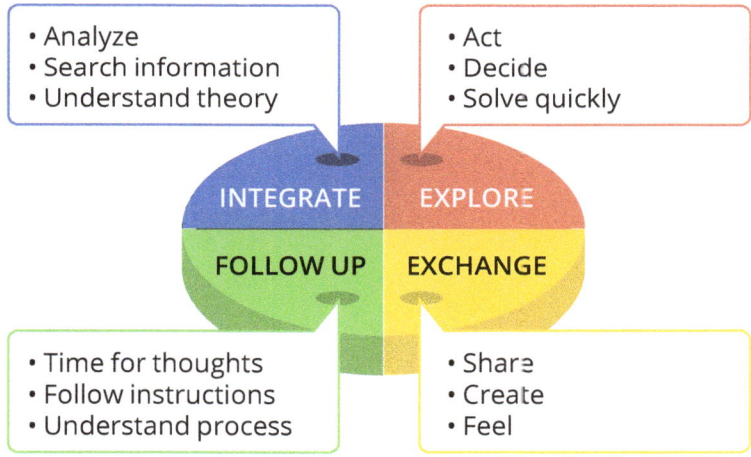

ACTION:

When learning, be aware of your dominant colour in a given moment. You may show the child where you are on the compass in order for them to model the way to learn.

---

54   Eric Kandel, born in 1929, an Australian-American medical doctor who won the Nobel Prize for his work on the physiological basis of memory storage in neurons.

# TIME TO WONDER

Would you agree that your learning preference is often your teaching one?

Create Colourful Pedagogical Capsules[55]

For Jean Houssaye, professor of educational sciences at the University of Rouen and head of the university's CIVIIC Laboratory, there is no teaching method in itself that fits all learners. For this reason, it is important to alternate pedagogical sequences by colours. To appreciate that everyone acquires knowledge differently is to accept and propose alternative modes of teaching for the same concept.

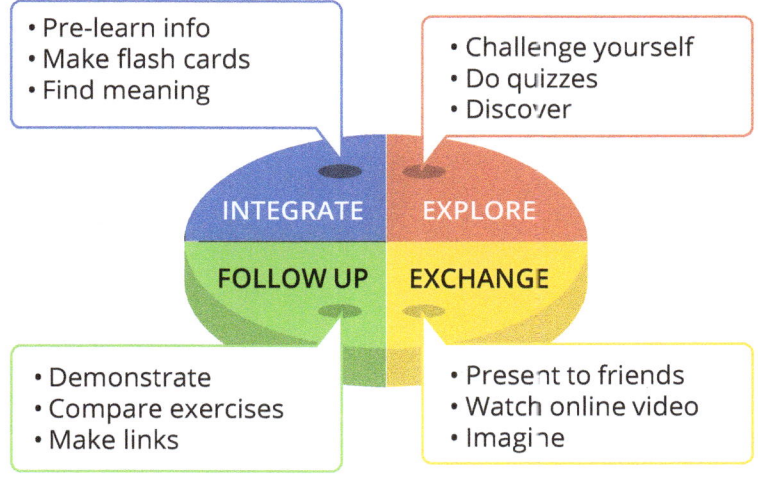

This second compass could be used at home, and was co-created via a virtual meeting with Celine Gagey, an amazing French middle school English educator.

---

55 Based on the Funny Learning approach from Brigitte Boussuat.

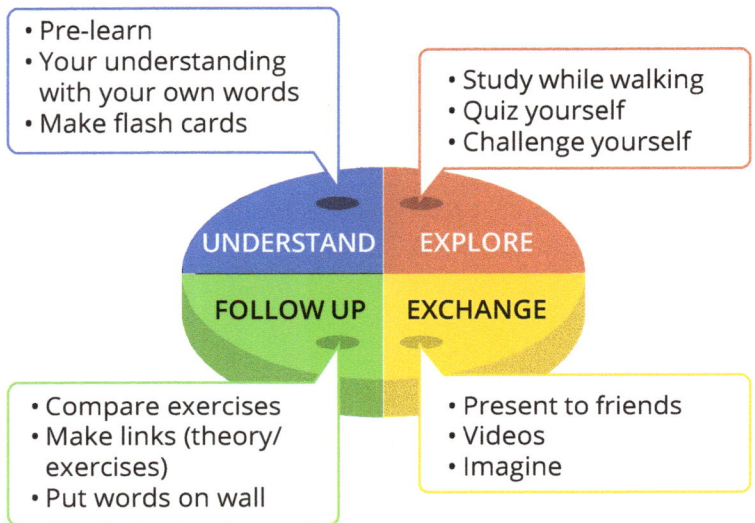

ACTION:

The colours will be explicitly presented to children in order to bring awareness to their own learning. Educators will design guided practice. Little by little, children will become aware of their needs as they become more proficient in recognizing their current colours and independently apply them.

This pedagogical approach requires us to:

Clarify the intention of a learning sequence: to set a clear objective (red), to make children interact (yellow), to anchor the learner's reality (green), and to structure and lay the foundations (blue). Initially, clear expectations and explicit instruction will be presented by the educator. This colour system is also presented to parents. Gradually autonomous learning will occur.

Integrate biorhythms:[56]

Let's integrate chronobiology and phases of vigilance during the course of the day. That way, it is possible to organize time according to students' needs. Alternating colours can be used to put the body and mind into motion. For example, yellow capsules made of exchanges and games, or red ones such as educational walks, challenges, and commitments can be used to suit the students' needs at any given time.

Biorhythms by Funny Learning is the pedagogical approach from Brigitte Boussuat. For a collective session, here is an average example with a few possible learning capsules. Asking learners to create their own graph would be best.

Daytime concentration levels:

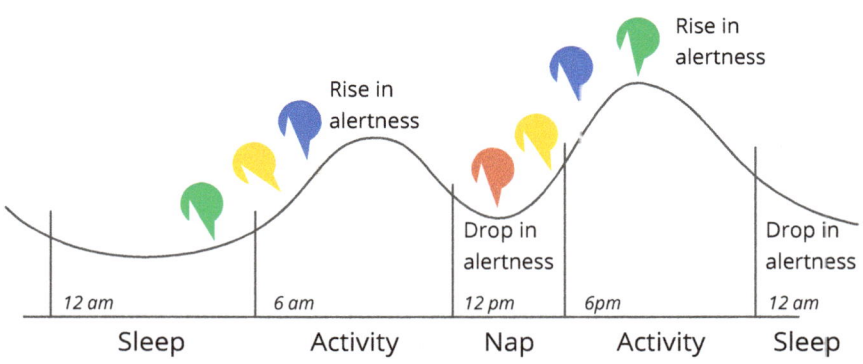

---

56   Funny Learning approach from Brigitte Boussuat.

This French example of the Daisy concept[57] could be offered to study at home through colours. Seven colourful micro activities could be given and the children choose the appropriate colour for them to study in on that day. Around the flower, you have the days of the week and the learner decides whether to really focus on understanding a topic in depth, share with someone a part of the topic, do some exercises, or explore the concept further through different approaches.

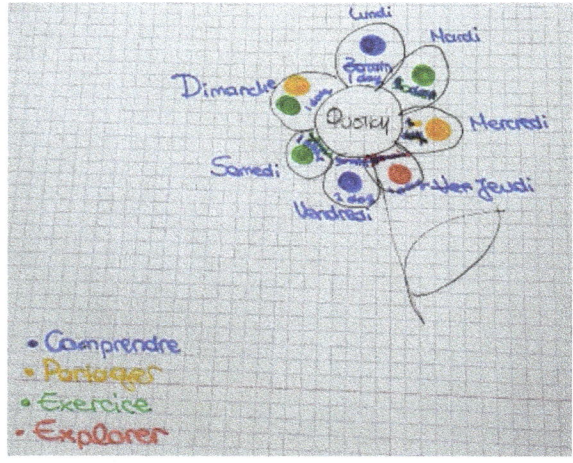

An example of the Daisy concept (in French) from a 15-year-old girl

The following page shows a possible example of a general group teaching quest after sending some learning content in advance (flipped learning):

---

57 Funny Learning approach from Brigitte Boussuat, author, speaker and trainer.

8: Consciousness

1 **PROJECTION**	2 **I WONDER**	3 **INTEGRATE**
Attitude, Objective, How? Why this topic? _____ mins	What do I know? What questions can I ask? Alone then two _____ mins	One idea (max three) + example(s) + link to their world. _____ mins
4 **TO CONNECT**	5 **FOLLOW UP**	6 **AN ENERGIZER**
Mental impression break and then time to share. I recall _____ mins	Collective design: Make visible links between theory and the learners' experiences & exercises. I reflect _____ mins	Video, a guest, story for a more concrete link and some inspiration with content. _____ mins
7 **EXPLORER**	8 **THE PRACTICAL CLUB**	9 **ACTION**
We practice and explore; theory in practice. _____ mins	I practice with someone or my team. What do I discover? _____ mins	Summary of lesson + gratitude time + actions to put in place. _____ mins

Learning Phases

Joseph Ledoux coined the expression *nomadic memory* to illustrate the long journey of memory and its mnemonic trace in our brain.[58] In order to be able to remember information after several years, there must have been multiple synaptic changes and therefore multiple opportunities to remember the same information over time. Salman Kahn promulgates the reverse pedagogy, which, by integrating ICTs, makes it possible to extend the duration of exposure to learning.

ACTIONS:
Integrating the learning into three phases to suit all learners: pre-learning online, the learning in classroom through colours, and post-learning online. Pre-learning flipped content could be the way to start the learning journey.

You can also imagine your classroom in colours like Marie Legrand did:

- A red space to explore content quickly. Learners who go fast may like to be alone, to be standing, to be autonomous. They like to have a timer and a board to write down their scores.

- A yellow space to exchange and take pleasure together. Learners who like to wander may like to be on the floor with access to a lot of material to create mind maps or creative content.

---

58   Joseph Ledoux, psychologist and professor in sciences at New York University and director of the Centre for the Neuroscience of Fear and Anxiety.

8: Consciousness

- A green space to follow up and take time to observe. Learners who like having some time may like to be sitting on big cushions or on sofas with another friend. No timer necessary in this green space, but a board that shows the way to learn and how to succeed is beneficial.

- The blue space to integrate brings method and rigor. Learners who like to go into details could be alone with some material. They need resources with rules, theories, or vocabulary lists to understand the "why" and the "how," and one activity after another with levels and free time management. Noise cancelling headphones and flash cards can also be provided.

Connection

Connect With the Learners

Psychologist Carol Dweck defines motivation as "the love of learning, the love of challenge."[59] According to her, motivation is often more important than initial ability in determining our success. Giving support, expressing emotional concerns, communicating with students to find strengths through a growth mindset, talking about failure, and providing incentives through clear projection and autonomous work ethic will encourage students' motivation. Creating an engaging classroom partnership will be beneficial for the child's motivation.

Remote Obstacles

The hippocampus (centre of memory) is equipped with numerous cortisol receptors (the stress hormone) which impact memory. The experiments conducted by Martin Seligman have demonstrated the notion of *learned helplessness*,[60] which completely inhibits the person

---

59   Carol Dweck, Mindset, the New Psychology of Success

60   The learned helplessness theory was conceptualized and developed by Martin Seligman, American psychologist at the University of Pennsylvania.

who is confronted by it, thus making them lose all hope of changing things, including learning new things. According to David Rock, educators can create a nurturing learning environment by underlining improvement especially when learning something new.[61] Then, presenting clear outlines of what will be learned and giving some autonomy through choice, fairness, and trust will remove obstacles.

99% of our brain's activity takes place without our knowledge. To understand our moods and *background thoughts*, as Christophe André put it,[62] is to identify the emotions which fundamentally influence thoughts and actions. This awareness programs the mind to open up and succeed.

ACTIONS:
It is therefore essential, before starting a lesson, that each student becomes aware of their feelings or energy regarding the objectives and content of the training. A wall of obstacles with sticky notes can also be written to help students move forward. More importantly, start with something the learners can do easily and, when they say that it is normal because it is easy, let them know that there is no easy exercise but only what is perceived to be easy because the skills have already been acquired. Show them how far they have come and remind them that it is about how they get to the outcome with good tools that will allow them to succeed. They will then create experiences and new references. So, starting with small steps with what they know will

---

61   David Rock, director of the Neuroleadership Institute, research from neuroscientists and leadership experts to build a new science for leadership development. [Rock, David. "The neuroscience of leadership." PhD diss., Middlesex University, 2010.]

62   Christophe André, *States of soul: An apprenticeship in serenity*, 2009.

encourage them to remove obstacles. Becoming good at something is possible through engaged trials.

In a group, some learning capsules (short learning sequences) to help the learners project positively in the learning can be used. You can show them the power of visualisation and the difficulty involved in changing habits. There is a very simple way to show them how hard it can be to change: ask them to cross their arms and then look around to check if everyone is doing the same thing. Then ask them to cross their arms the other way around. It usually takes awhile for the brain to adapt and change its habitual way of arm crossing. Some questions to create relatedness and curiosity could also be asked to help remove fear.

Active Listening and Feedforward

To enable a dialogue to happen, Carl Rogers' active listening is essential because it builds strong and effective communication with the learner. The educator will then become a facilitator, fully concentrating on, engaging in, and being absorbed by what the learner is projecting. It is not the facilitator of knowledge giving a piece of advice to the learner, but it is an engagement through active listening that will allow the learner to find their own personal learning journey. It is more an *equal meeting* in which the learner and the facilitator will collaborate. Carl Rogers' principles are non-judgement, empathy, and congruence. The attitude of the educator needs to be awareness of self and acceptance of differences, with the ability to let go of limiting beliefs. It is important to point out that there is a plethora of individual approaches to learning. There are essential learning processes for everyone. These begin with projection, i.e., what and how they are learning, and the feelings associated with it. The learners can then question themselves about their "mind's content and procedures" for a successful learning task to happen.

ACTIONS:
Feedforward helps learners avoid mental shut down, reinforces positive behaviour, and helps them focus on development rather than ratings.

Here are four steps used by David Rock in Neuroleadership:

> **Step One:**
> Are you ready to debrief your learning?
>
> **Step Two:**
> What are the three things you felt you did well? Would it be ok if I shared my observations of what you did well?
>
> **Step Three:**
> What would you like to do differently next time?
>
> **Step Four:**
> Add your own thoughts about areas of development.

Positive Emotions

A vast majority of the students who choose to drop out of the French school system each year blame a lack of motivation as a leading cause. If it is closely linked to Part 1 (lack of "personalisation" of the pedagogy), it is also due to an unattractive pedagogy made up of set pedagogical outlines, obligations, and sanctions, often triggering passive or rebellious behaviour. The brain is exploratory by nature and hates being bored. The pedagogy of discovery, of which Célestin Freinet was a major contributor, makes the learner a driving force and an active participant. This requires a change in the educators' role (Freinet at the time advocated removing "the stage"). The teacher is not the knower who *distributes* knowledge, they are a facilitator and provide access to knowledge, they are the guide of a space in which everyone must feel at home.

ACTIONS:

- Changing the organization of spaces with round tables, a teacher circulating in the middle of the group, and organizing through a colour system when possible: green for a quieter place to reflect, blue for a place to read documents and understand theories, yellow for a place to exchange and connect with peers to explain children's understanding, and red as a place to explore and test yourself, with scores to be motivated. If the colour system can't be put in place within the classroom, you can create a colourful journey and clearly state the colour to the children.

- Creating spaces of learning (like the colour space explained earlier) that are often changed, such as using themed walls for visual reminders. I remember creating a special *Get on the Plane* experience to prepare first-year secondary students for a French oral test. On my door the AIR FRANCE sign hung, welcoming students on board a plane, and a quick refurbishing of my classroom on the inside made the experience more immersive. A trolley was used to bring the conversation topics to the students, as if they were being given a menu on a real plane or had to engage in new conversation with their neighbours.

- Welcoming with music according to the topic of the day. For example, I remember playing the opening of the Rocky Balboa theme song to practice for the IGCSE French exams!

- Creating caring spaces that are positive communication stations. The brain gravitates towards what pleases it and tends to avoid pain.

- Moving stations, where children can learn verbs or math through movement. Imagine that you can learn verbs on a carpet with colours, numbers, and dice.

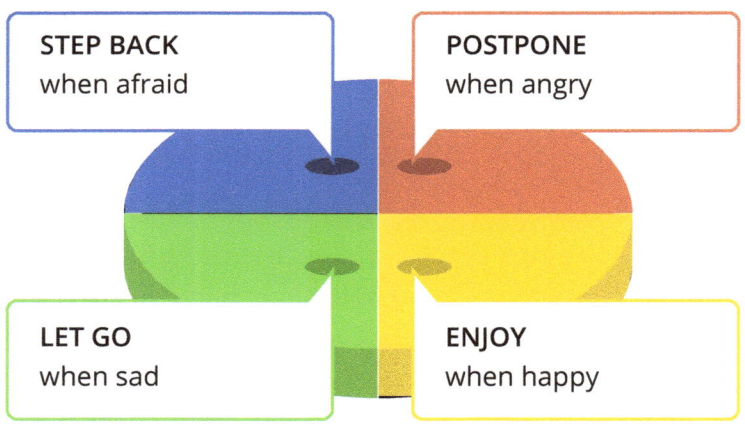

Emotions (positive or negative) enhance memory because they encourage the brain to pay attention, as highlighted by James Papez. A lot of adults will remember what they did on September 11, 2001, because the high emotional intensity of this event may have left chemical and electrical markers in the brain. Exploiting the stimuli that generate emotions means triggering laughter, joy, nostalgia, frustration, or even fear in the learner. A short video icebreaker is a capsule that can quickly provide this effect. Moving from emotion to action is being mindful of your emotion and its sensation, then naming the feeling and what it needs to let the learner be able to go towards action. The learner can decide on possible actions and explain why this is happening. Some colourful spaces or chairs could be placed to express the emotional state learners are in.

"Projection"

Antoine de la Garanderie, author of *Mental Management* and philosopher of the 20th century, wrote about enabling explorations of our mental habits and processes that he calls *mental gestures*. This triangle enhances awareness of what and how children move forward towards learning, optimizing successful mental strategies, and allowing transfer to areas of difficulty. Students' engagement at this stage is essential to ensure a positive learning progression.

Thierry Janssen says that "growth is only possible when it is necessary."[63] Learners who take ownership of their learning and are immersed in their process, with an awareness of the possible gains, will be able to project themselves towards success. This is how personalized learning processes can occur in a classroom.

---

63   From *Your brain has not finished surprising you* by Boris Cyrulnik.

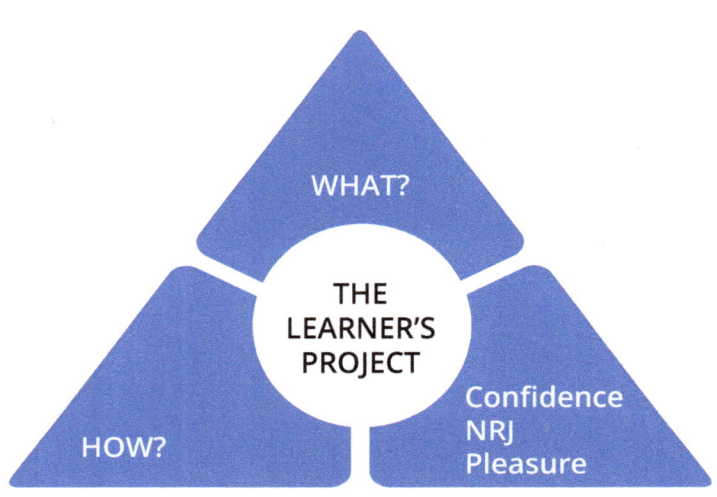

ACTION:
You can share your own triangle and ask learners to create one of their own.

10
Curiosity
From Teaching to Facilitating

Curiosity, autonomy, and critical thinking promote the development of a child's personality. Curiosity stimulates and creativity encourages the child's curiosity. The notion of creativity generally refers to a child's ability to express their own personality. A neurological study has shown that curiosity makes brains more receptive to learning, and that as children learn, they enjoy the sensation of learning. Curiosity is a form of intrinsic motivation that is key to fostering active learning. Educators play a critical role in helping students transform their curiosity into inquiry, by facilitating, focusing, challenging, and encouraging students in active engagement.[64]

ACTIONS:
Perhaps the idea of getting your students out of their seats seems scary to you, but by introducing more movement and discussion to your classroom, you are inviting new interests, passion, and a sense of community. There are so many strategies (see a few on the following page) that are easy to implement. You will definitely see the difference

---
64   Zion & Slezak, 2005.

in your students' energy levels, and see that this way of learning is worthwhile.

- Pair up and exchange
- Energizers
- Cross-laterals gym
- Group work
- Role plays
- Quick games
- Short colour capsules

Thiagi's[65] facilitating work also keeps the learners totally absorbed, as well as being practical and fun. You can find many ideas online from thiagi.com. Dr Sivailam, the founder of the Thiagi Group, was a high school science teacher and a college professor in his early life.

A few possible capsules

A few possible capsules with two different energies. You can indeed mix the colours to bring different energy in and you can even bring all the different colours in if you wish to work through all of the different ones. According to the need of the moment, you can choose the energies you wish for your group.

"In two minutes, when I say go, you will stand"

---

[65] Dr. Sivasailam "Thiagi" Thiagarajan, founder of Thiahi Group, an organization that improves performance effectively and enjoyably, author of several books, researcher, speaker, and college professor.

1. Remember

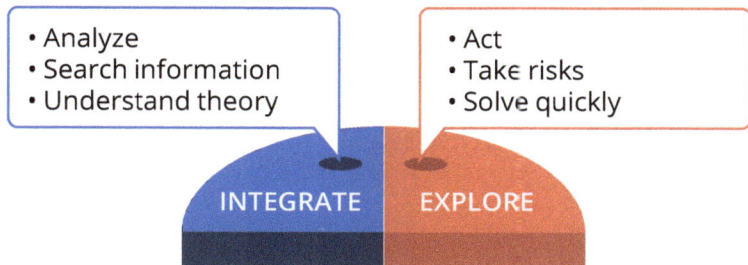

After presenting new knowledge, you feel that your learners need to retain it. With these two colours, learners can check their understanding and explore how to memorize it through a creative context. It will bring understanding and action together towards a result: remembering.

Objective: Memorisation and creativity.

Ready: One post-it note with one key word from the learning session.

Steady: Read the sticky notes and take some time to create your mental impression. Explore with your eyes or move around the room and decide on one object in your classroom that you would associate with your word. It could also be outside the classroom.

Go: Come back to your seat and in 5-10 minutes, write a short story of the alliance of the word and the object.

Debrief: The day after, check how much you remember. The week after, how much do you remember?

2. Let's get together

FOLLOW UP
- Time for thoughts
- Follow instructions
- Understand process

EXCHANGE
- Share
- Create
- Feel

After presenting new knowledge, you feel that your learners need to consolidate it. With these two colours, learners can reflect and exchange about their learning. It will bring reflection and action together as well as build relationships within the group.

Objective: Memorising and communicating.

Ready: Big paper board sheets with a pen per learner. Sheets can be either on the floor or on the walls.

Steady: You will take all the notes that you have taken and create a collective mind map.

Go:
- Explain the mind map concept
- Action plan before starting
- Everyone needs to participate

Debrief: How did sharing help you reflect on what had been said? Did you create new meanings?

3. Feedback gift

After presenting new knowledge, you feel that your learners need more insights. With these two colours, learners can reflect more deeply about their learning. It will bring reflection on a piece of theory and an exercise that has been linked to it.

- Analyze
- Search information
- Understand theory

INTEGRATE

FOLLOW UP

- Time for thoughts
- Follow instructions
- Understand process

Objective: Giving feedback and bringing consciousness.

Ready: Prepare 3 cards:
- First card, feedback 1: What do you like about the other's work?
- Second card, feedback 2: What could be improved?
- Third card, feedback 3: What have you learned from them?

Steady: Learners have finished an exercise and they give each other their work. The first piece of feedback is about what the learner likes about the other's work, the second piece of feedback is about something that could be improved in the exercise, and the last one starts with sharing, "What I have learnt from you" and a thank you.

Go: The learners start alone for 5 to 10 minutes and read through the three cards. The learners pair up and start the process.

Debrief: Becoming conscious of sharing through observation of each other's work. How did this feedback help you reflect on what you have done? Did you create new meaning?

4. Facing a problem

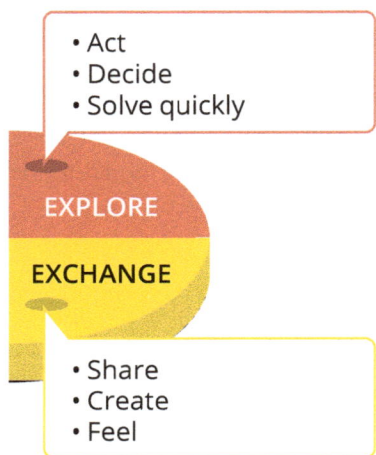

After presenting new knowledge, you feel that your learners are stuck on what has been learnt. Stop with this capsule for a moment. With these two colours, learners can be in action; thoughts usually come with action. It will enable your learners to step "outside" of a problem for a few minutes and bring the creative energy in.

Objective: Solutions & creativity.

Ready: Build a stack of things in the classroom.

Steady: Tell your learners that they need to imagine how to get to the other side of the wall without copying the strategy of the others in the classroom.

Go: Either they write down all the possibilities or they actually try to get to the other side of the wall. This can be done outside the classroom.

Debrief: Representing an obstacle mentally is essential. Some will think of doing it head on (red), some will find loopholes to go through (green), some will analyse piece by piece how to deconstruct the stack (blue), or others will go around the big way or ask others to help (yellow). By imagining that this stack is some of the difficulties you can face, what have you learnt about it?

5. Recalling information

After presenting new knowledge, you feel that your learners need to be aware of what they know and what they need to work on. Stop 10 minutes before the end of your session and try this capsule. With these two colours, learners can reflect and be in action. It will also allow you, as an educator, to see where your learners stand.

Objective: Recalling information and getting feedback from the group.

Ready: Three different colour sticky notes.

Steady: At the end of a session or a learning week, invite learners to fill in the sticky notes with one or more words.
1.   I feel (physically, intellectually, or emotionally)
2.   I recall
3.   I need

Go: Each of the participants, before leaving the room, should write a comment on each of the rubrics.

Debrief: A synthesis can be done by one learner or by the educator.

6. Let's move forward

Before presenting some new knowledge, you need to project your learners towards this new learning content, and you feel that they need some movement. You can prepare 10 questions in advance and try this capsule. With these two colours, learners can reflect and be in action to let everyone know how they feel about learning this piece of knowledge. It will also allow you to see, as an educator, where your learners stand.

Objective: Understanding motivation.

Ready: Prepare about 10 questions and make sure to have enough space along an imaginary line.

Steady: Tell the learners to take a spot on one of the endpoints that suits their answer. They can't be in the middle or outside the line.

Go: Ask a question that offers two possible answers (one for each endpoint): Do you prefer working alone or in a group? Do you know the topic we are going to learn: yes or no? How confident are you in your knowledge about the topic: 1 or 10? Do you like that topic: yes or no?

Debrief: What have you learnt about yourself? And others?

These capsules will activate mind, body, and heart: They will enable learners some movement while learning, and learners will also become more aware of how they learn. Movement is essential to learning and therefore a learning session should always bring some motion. The first evidence of a link between mind and body was scattered in various proposals over the past century.[66] Today, most neuroscientists agree that movement and cognition are powerfully connected.

Activate Mind, Body, and Heart

Descartes promoted dualism between the noble soul and the machine body.[67] Schools and universities have developed static learning models that have recently been challenged by neuroscience. Neuroscientists have discovered that the provision of additional oxygen brings a significant improvement in cognitive faculties. Dr. Yancey recommends physical education twice a day.[68]

Emotional regulation and awareness in the daily lives of children and educators is crucial. Studies on the brain confirm the place emotions have in learning, and it's not just a matter of well-being that reinforces motivation and work capacity. According to the authors of "Emotions at the heart of the learning process," published in the *Neuroscience and Special Education Journal*, "the same [brain] region can be characterized as 'cognitive' or 'emotional' in learning.

---

66   Schmahmann, 1997.

67   In the philosophy of mind from René Descartes (1596–1650), mind-body dualism denotes that the mind and body are separable.

68   Asa G. Yancey Sr, (1916-2013) American physician professor emeritus from the Emory University School of Medicine.

Emotions and cognitive processes thus mobilize identical areas of the brain."[69]

ACTIONS:
Some specific capsules (yellow/red) can provide some energy that can be activated at times of low alertness, either at the start of the day or after lunch, according to what the students want. The brain needs physical exercise to be active so let's activate it through movement. For example, you could learn French verbs by putting many sheets of infinitive verbs on the floor, a die for the personal pronouns (I is one dot, you singular is two dots, he/she/it is three dots…) and tenses can be chosen by the students. You can display some words on the wall and choose to play a song for a listening task: as you play the song, children need to get up and pick up the word they hear. For a review purpose, you can hide some boxes in the classroom and in teams, children will have to answer the question they find inside the box.

Iteration and Collaboration

The concept of Agility comes from Agile learning and is also used in the world of technology. When agile teams collaborate on projects, they give ongoing feedback and make sure to take care of minor obstacles before they become major ones. If they notice that there is something wrong, they change plan. Agile methodology is more and more applied in the world of higher education since the agile learning approach uses the idea of mistakes as a learning tool. It also makes learners accountable for their actions. They are encouraged to try again when they fail;

---

69 Mary Helen Immordino-Yang & Antonio Damasio, "We Feel, Therefore We Learn: The Relevance of Affective and Social Neuroscience to Education," *Mind Brain and Education,* March 2007.

this is what the iterative process is about. They give it a go, fail, learn and start again. Thus, educators can observe where learners might need extra guidance.

ACTIONS:
When learners use an agile learning approach, they are given a task or a project for a specific time — it could be one class or a week, for example. Those short periods of time are called sprints; after each of them, learners reflect on what has been done and improve when necessary, reorganize their tasks or even change their plan. When a sprint finishes, another one starts. A board (a Kanban)[70] can measure progress thanks to a whiteboard and sticky notes or even a digital version that would have the same objective. When learners work together, they can keep an eye on their progress through three columns: to do, in progress and done. Learners can therefore make choices on how they wish to learn and become both responsible and engaged in their own learning.

The Power of Questioning to the Development of Critical Thinking

According to neuroscientists, the prefrontal cortex is responsible for the combined questioning and critical thinking that underline inquiry. When students can project themselves through initiatives, goals, plans, and integrating information, they use their prefrontal cortex.[71] When the questions are asked, power is on! Students ask more questions and become active learners, taking ownership of the inquiry.

---

70 A visual workflow management tool; see https://kanbanize.com/kanban-resources/getting-started/what-is-kanban

71 Fleming 2010.

For me, questions are not only a channel into the learners' thoughts, they are the seeds of thought itself. Starting with what learners already know is inviting them to challenge their knowledge and engage with the learning. Albert Einstein said once, "If I had an hour to solve a problem and my life depended on the solution, I would spend the first 55 minutes determining the proper question to ask."[72] Asking questions that students want to know activates an internal desire for action (called *intrinsic motivation*). Asking starts with not knowing but wanting to know: Piaget[73] called it *disequilibrium*. The child's discomfort in not knowing sets curiosity and inquiry in motion. If learning consists of exploring and making sense of things, then questioning is the call to action that can start the learning process. Wonder is also what works best since questioning will fuel wonder. When questions come from children, they will more likely lead to further inquiry.

---

72   Albert Einstein is a German-born theoretical physicist who developed the theory of relativity and one of the two pillars of modern physics.

73   Jean Piaget, Swiss psychologist who made a systematic study of the acquisition of understanding in children. Equilibrium describes one of the four critical factors in cognitive development.

ACTIONS:
A few questions to be asked could be:

EXPLORE

- Can you predict the outcome?
- How could you improve the outcome?
- What evidence can you find?
- What questions could you be asked or ask yourself?

INTEGRATE

- Can you explain the main concept or idea in a paragraph?
- What facts will you select to show that you understand?
- How can you compare it (similar/different)?
- What, where, who, how, why?

 **EXCHANGE**

- What already exists (is searching online possible)?
- What changes would you make to solve the question?
- Can you use some information in a new way?
- Can you invent…?

 FOLLOW UP

- What facts will you select to show…?
- What approach will you use?
- How will you organize yourself to show that…?
- How would you apply what you have learnt in…?

11
Confidence
From Concentrating to Success

Learning how to learn is a metacognitive process that can be introduced: thinking about thinking and feelings. Metacognition enables learners to dive into their own way of learning. Developing awareness about their learning is an essential skill as they grow older because when learners cultivate metacognitive skills, they are able to check in with their thoughts and reframe their thinking in order to adapt to new situations. Learners can choose what works best for them since they have a better understanding of actions, rules and what is going on around them. They become more mindful of why some subjects might need longer hours of studies and even accept effort and mistakes.

Focus Attention

Considering that 90% of learners have forgotten what they have learned after 90 days,[74] making a memory last is one of the great tasks of learning. In the four phases of memorization (encoding, storage, recall or restitution, and forgetting), pedagogy has a primordial role in the first phase. Emotions (positive or negative) improve memory because they

---

74 Herman Ebbinghaus, *Memory: A Contribution to Experimental Psychology.*

encourage the brain to pay attention, as James Papez pointed out. As an example, when something life-changing happens, we are more likely to remember because emotions leave chemical and electrical markers. Exploiting emotion-generating stimuli triggers laughter, joy, nostalgia, frustration, and even fear in the learner. A short icebreaker video could be a pedagogical capsule to engage an emotional response.

ACTIONS:
Michael Posner developed a three-step theory of attention.[75] This approach uses these steps to create pedagogical hooks for:

1. Alert (something abnormal and unusual happens, attention is fixed). Bring a sign, a sound, or an image that would fix attention at a moment in time. You could raise your hand, clap or say a sentence, a word, or perform an unusual body or facial movement.

2. Direct attention (one can only have one conscious idea at a time). Sequencing according to the 10-minute rule: 1 minute to explain the concept (meaning), 9 minutes of detail, followed by an icebreaker.

3. Execute (for the learner to get involved in the action, for example). You can bring something fun or unexpected (yellow), calm music with a video (green), a graph and unexpected numbers (blue), or a challenge (red).

---

75 Michael I. Posner, American psychologist, author of numerous cognitive and neuroscience compilations, and an eminent researcher in the field of attention. Emeritus professor of psychology at the University of Oregon.

11: Confidence

How to Be Attentive[76]

In your life, you may have heard this many times: "Be more attentive!" But what do we really need to do? Attention is a *mind activity*; it is the act of making an object become present in the mind, as a mental image, a picture, a sound, and/or a sensation. Attention while reading a text or listening to a song is determined by what is taking place in the mind. And, to do so, you need to accomplish a specific intent or project: imagination, in this step, will enable the learner to be more curious and aware of what is happening in their mind.

You can help parents understand how to help the child in the process of being attentive by asking the following questions at home.

Learning How to Learn: **Questions to be more attentive:**
What is your objective? What are you going to use it for? How will you do it and how do you feel?

In this step, creating some space for imagination will enable the learner to be more curious and aware of what can be happening in their mind.

ACTIONS:
Give the learner time to prepare before starting, and give the learner time to check their mental impression. Also, only activate one perception at a time: if you show something, don't talk. If you talk, don't show. We tend to use all the perceptions at the same time.

---

76 Antoine de la Garanderie, a French philosopher and pedagogue, and founder of the mental management theory that describes precisely the mental mechanisms when learning.

Attention is the first step to learning:

1. *Project*: what is your project? Your objective? How will you do it? How do you feel?

2. *Perception*: Look, listen, touch, feel ...

3. *Mental impression*:[77] How does this lesson impress upon your mind?

Boost Memorization (a Complex Encapsulation)

Alan Baddeley describes working memory as a three-dimensional model: auditory, visual, and phonological.[78] We now know that the more complex we encode information, the more durable the engram will be. The use of examples allows us to connect new information to other memories already in place and to encourage long-term anchoring and consolidation. Hermann Ebbinghaus demonstrated the relevance of repetition cycles and spaced learning.[79] A large part of our memories fades two hours after exposure. The implementation of short repetition loops (three reminders of 10 minutes each) improves memorization by going back to the same concept in a different way. The remainder can be done by group play, topographic memorization, and collective mind mapping, thereby allowing the three capsules to make the conversation between the cortex and the hippocampus last, and to generate a

---

[77] Antoine de la Garanderie uses the word "evocation."
[78] Alan Baddeley is British psychologist known for his research on memory and for developing the three-component model of working memory.
[79] Herman Ebbinghaus, *Memory: A Contribution to Experimental Psychology.*

long-term potentiation (PLT).

How Does the Memorisation[80] Process Work?

Memorisation begins with attention. This step requires many movements back and forth between perceptions and mind, with the intention to use the information in the future. Encoding can be done through a clear project, either chronologically, spatially, or through movement in the mind. Recalling will then be easier. Repeating can be done through a change of perception (visual, auditory, or kinaesthetic) but if there is *no project*, repetition will not enable a recall of information or reconstruction of knowledge. Imagining the future of when this knowledge will be needed can enable the reconstruction of knowledge or evocation to vary and enable this step to be successful. Imagination here is also enabling the creation of original ways to encode and recall information in the future. And according to neuroscience, ongoing evocation is essential: after an hour, a day, a week, a month, and a term.

You can help parents understand how to help the child in the process of memorizing by going through the following questions at home.

Learning How to Learn: Questions to enable the memorization process:

How are you going to keep this piece of knowledge in your mind...? Explain to me how you do it.

Where will you need this knowledge? When will you need it? Will you

---

80   Antoine de la Garanderie.

still remember it tonight/tomorrow/when being questioned? Imagine yourself in a situation of restitution…

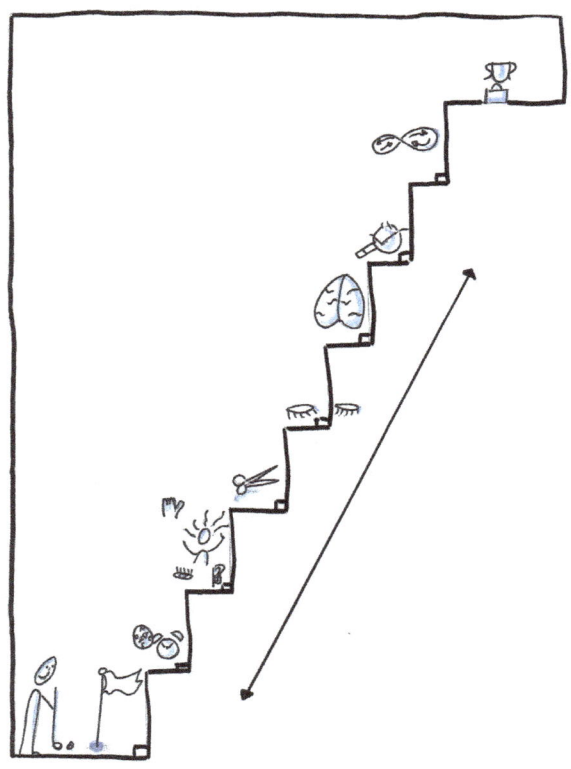

A picture version of the memorization process, a collaborative work with a 12-year-old boy, Leo.

11: Confidence

ACTION:

Clearly show the learners what steps to take, and when facilitating the process, ask the learner where they are in the process?

Here are the steps to memorize:

1. *Project*: what is your project? Your objective? How will you do it? How do you feel?

2. When, where and how will I use it?

3. *Perception*: look, listen, touch.

4. *Chunk*: cut your learning into small pieces.

5. *Eyes closed:* no document in front of you. You can also move with your eyes open!

6. *Mental impression*: awareness of how the content is in your head.

7. *Check*: go back to your work, compare it to what is in your mind.

8. *Repeat*: after one hour, one day, one week, one month, one term, and one semester

You can ask the learner what step(s) are missing.

Facilitate Comprehension[81]

You might have said, "You don't understand this word?!" before, but how do you lead the learner to give their own answer?

The first step to comprehension is attention. To understand, *evocation* must occur; the *mind activity* needs to make links of comparison (similarities or differences) and some movement back and forth between perceptions and mind. It may happen that meaning comes intuitively, but sometimes there needs to be many movements between perceptions and mind; taking clues, giving hypotheses, and translating into our own words. The different ways to create meaning are either through a chronology of time, spatial organization, or movement in the mind. On top of those different ways, learners will either have a *meaningful* project to understand by transformation or by reproduction. Imagination here is important to change points of view and test your hypothesis.

You can help parents understand how to help the child in the process of comprehension by going through these questions at home:

***Learning How to Learn:* Questions to enable the comprehension process to happen:**
Where did you hear about this information? Can this information give you an idea of what this word means?

Compare this idea with your lesson and see if it fits. Are you sure that …? Look again with your new ideas. Does the meaning seem satisfactory to you now?

---

81   Antoine de la Garanderie.

What would be your hypothesis?

ACTION:
Clearly show the learners what steps to take, and when facilitating the process, ask the learner where they are in the process.

Here are the iterative steps needed to comprehend that could be used during the integration process.

What steps do you need to take?

1. *Project*: What is your project? Your objective? How will you do it? How do you feel?

2. *Perception*: look, listen, touch.

3. *Mental impression*: do you have an awareness of how it is in your head?

4. *Links*: make links with what you know.

5. *Check*: review the document again.

6. *Translation*: with your own words.

7. *Production*: write your understanding.

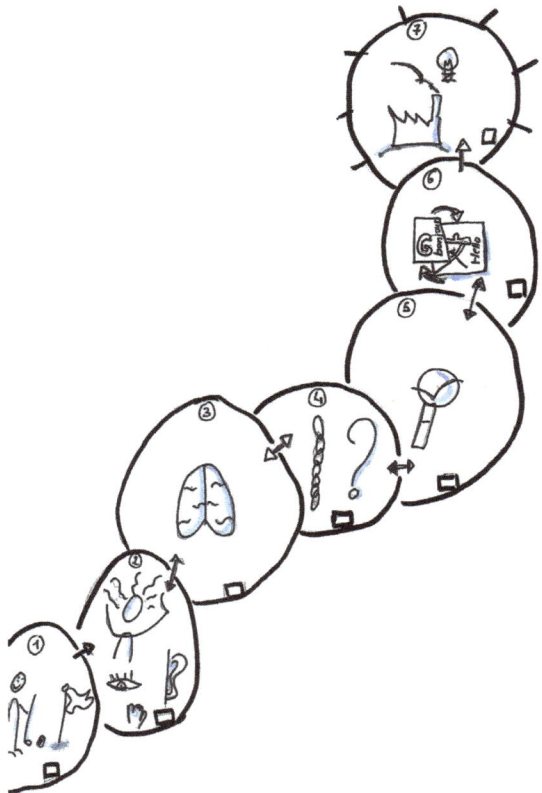

A picture of the comprehension process, a collaborative work with a 12-year-old boy, Leo.

Stimulate Reflection[82] (Thinking Back)

You must have heard this many times: "You can't think!" but how do you lead the learner towards thinking without telling them what thinking really is?

---

82   Antoine de la Garanderie, Réussir, ça s'apprend.

Reflection is an act which ventures into past knowledge (acquired knowledge), bringing it to the forefront, in order to question what needs to be reflected upon. Therefore, having evocations of past knowledge will activate reflection. The sorting of knowledge is required in the reflection process. Learning to anticipate this reflection will trigger accurate reflection in the future. It is a *recalling of acquired knowledge* or a *flexion back in the past*. This step works hand in hand with the memorization step, and by consolidated comprehension and imagination. During this step, you can imagine what original tools could be adapted, transformed, or invented to solve a problem.

You can help parents understand how to help the child in the process of reflecting by going through the following questions at home.

Learning How to Learn: **Reflecting questions to enable the thinking process to occur:**
What is this with your own words? Does that mean anything to you?

What do you know about this? How can you connect these two pieces of information to the knowledge you know?

What do you conclude from this?

Next time you have a question like this, how are you going to do it?

ACTION:
Clearly show the learners what steps to take, and when facilitating the process, ask the learners where they are in the process.

Here are the iterative steps to reflect that could be done in the follow-up process:

What steps do you need to take?

1. *Project*: what is your project? Your objective? How will you do it? How do you feel?

2. *Perception*: look, listen, touch.

3. *Mental impression*: be aware of how it is in your head.

4. *Translating problems*: choose your words and sentences to explain.

5. *Check*: go back to the initial document.

6. *Selecting and sorting out*: Check your prior knowledge and choose what would be useful in the process.

7. *Solution*: what is it?

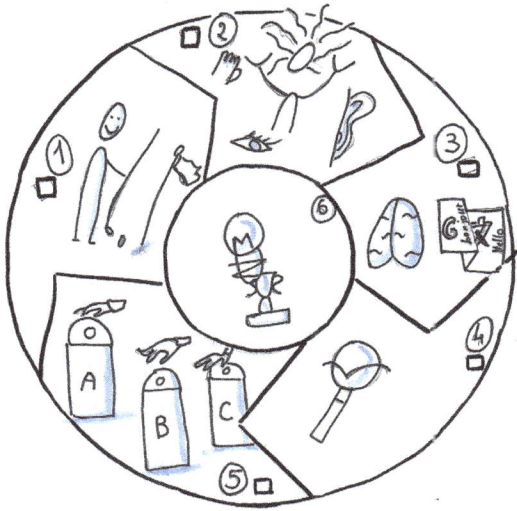

A picture version of the reflection process, a collaborative work with a 12-year-old boy, Leo.

Liberate the Imagination[83]

Imagination is an act that you will find in all the other steps. It reveals a project that is meaningful for the learner with the purpose of evoking the original object of perception. Evoking can be done as a discoverer, meaning that the learner will need everything they know and to test what they don't yet know. They will need to know why things are the way they are. Whereas the inventor will bring creations that exist already and compare them to their imagination to find something that doesn't exist yet. This learner will need to figure out how to do it in their own way. One learner will be happy to invent a story and another one will

---

83   Marie-Pierre Gallien, Ph.D., former teacher, trainer, and speaker, author of *Libérer l'imagination* and *Apprendre en couleurs*.

be happy to start from a text and add to it. Let's welcome what doesn't exist and take pleasure in what can be imagined. When the children can't find the answer, let them make some hypothesis.

ACTION:
In a music class for example, you could let children listen to some jazz music and let them imagine some new musicians, erase some instruments from the audio, substitute a quick rhythm for a slow one, or even change the solo clarinet to a solo guitar.

When facilitating the process of imagination, ask the learner some of the following questions.

Learning How to Learn: **Questions could be:**

- How do you...?
- What purpose...?
- Tell me ...
- Think about ...
- It may be a good idea, what do you think?
- What other idea could you bring?

12
Communication
From Sharing Strengths to Everybody's Success

A dialogue deepens learners' understanding of an issue or topic by sparking engaged learning through an open exchange of perspectives. The dialogue process encourages those involved to analyse course content, it inspires reflection, and it stimulates inclusivity in the classroom. It can also be a journey of discovery within the five *Learning How to Learn* steps through questioning: Attention is the initial *Learning How to Learn* step and the essential first step into the remaining learning steps: memorizing, understanding, reflecting, and using creative imagination to invent or discover new possibilities. The four-colour compass can be shared with parents in order to create a common language at home and at school.

A Sustainable Ecosystem
The global challenges we are facing today have a complexity that we have never faced before. They affect every nation, every person, and every aspect of our planet and even beyond. Growing a sustainable ecosystem of learners involves connecting home, school, and work.

Individuals are connected to content experts, enrolled in mentoring programs, and supported by peer-to-peer systems. This may lead to the creation of system thinkers[84] who appreciate the interactions between the elements that compose the entire system. System thinking is by nature metacognitive and with tools to reflect, children will grow in their emotional and social lives. The key systems thinking components are: multiple perspectives, interconnection, influences, and boundaries.

ACTIONS:
The tools for working together include facilitation, informal conversations, active listening, meetings, and some wonder cafes (a café where we could wonder) between parents and children to create some collective inspirations.

It requires clear intention from the beginning: how do I want my child to succeed? What result am I expecting from this meeting? What is my promise to live fully in this moment? What are we trying to understand? What are we trying to create? What will it be like when we achieve this purpose?

Step 1:
Define what works already for the child (strengths).

Step 2:
Define the difficulty and the necessary outcome.

---

84 Systems thinking is a holistic approach to analysis that focuses on the way that a system's constituent parts interrelate.

Step 3:
Co-create a possible transfer from difficulty to possibility into positive actions.

Step 4:
Design an action using the new learning; the community can share what works for them as inspiration (not as pieces of advice).

Create a Constellation of Support

Designing and managing a support system is a vital part of this approach, as well as finding accountable buddies that could move engagement to another level. If we think of implementing the Mindgility® program (agility of mind for children) in the transition from primary to secondary school, it will support the child's adjustment from a smaller, caring school environment with few educators, to large and relatively impersonal ones with multiple educators. This will help create a developmental match at a time when relationships with close, supportive adults are needed.[85]

ACTIONS:
Students need to recognize and identify people who can provide guidance and support. I usually create a map with a star system, helping them identify who can help when difficulty arises.

Multiply Interactions

Setting clear communicative expectations and showing learners how

---

85   Luthar & Ciciolla, 2016.

to be agile communicators both inside and outside the classroom will encourage everyone to interact positively with one another. This communicative approach[86] is the pedagogical representation of Jung and Marston's work on human behaviour, and thanks to this compass, children, parents, and educators will be able to navigate the world of communication and appropriately identify the colour of the speaker and respond accordingly.

In the blue zone, it is important to deliver facts and high-quality work. In the yellow, the drivers are feelings and a good relationship with others. In red, it is the world of action and it is better to do, even if starting over is necessary. In green, it is the world of calmness and taking time to reflect.

---

[86] The 4Colors approach by Brigitte Boussuat.

12: Communication

[Blue box]

Be precise, factual and structured.

Introduce and present the subject before we start to talk.

Indicate how much time will be needed.

Take time to go into details.

Stay distant, no touching.

Don't rush.

Keep a realistic approach and be measured without being scattered.

[Orange box]

Outline the objectives.

Be concise and asserted.

Go straight to the point if you feel impatient.

Enhance what they can learn by following your point.

Enhance challenge.

Lead them to decide.

Make them move if possible.

[Green box]

Be empathetic.

Create true relationships.

Take time to build trust.

Don't expose the person by asking their opinion but help them decide.

Be patient and build confidence.

[Yellow box]

Show your enthusiasm and warm rapport.

Share your pleasurable moments and let them speak.

Be creative and informal.

Show them what you appreciate in them.

Share dreams with them.

Get off-topic and come back to it later.

When presenting the idea for clarifying thoughts in conflicts, opening the discussion to the floor is likely to bring out ideas and reactions from parents.

The magnifying glasses below are used when there is a conflict in a group. First, learners write their ideas individually and then share them within the group. They need to look at the facts (each of the learners should write them down) and their own perceptions (which of course are usually their personal understanding of the issue) before going into action. Learners can therefore share their facts and perceptions first and then exchange their solutions to choose the one that can help them all move forward.

Here is an example co-created at the École Montessori Schule Hobsheid between myself, an educator (Lara), and a parent:

FACTS

WHAT ARE THE FACTS?

12: Communication

PERCEPTIONS

WHAT HAVE YOU PERCEIVED?

SOLUTION

WHAT SOLUTION WOULD WORK FOR BOTH OF US?

IMAGINATION

WHAT CAN WE DO TO MAKE ENDS MEET?

ACTIONS:

When the learning stops because of communication problems, there are tasks we can ask young learners to do individually, then through interactions. This idea came while talking with an educator for primary learners (6–12 years old) and during an online conference for parents. The educator, Lara, had shared with me the communication difficulties she was facing in the classroom as well as her needs. She talked to me about the vision of what she believed could work within the classroom as well as outside the classroom. We both decided to share our idea with parents at an online evening conference. For me, parent conferences give a voice to educators who can show what has been done as well as sharing practical ideas to implement at home.

In a Nutshell

1. Consciousness: Go forward
In order to successfully navigate a classroom, it is important to know yourself as an educator as well as yourself as a learner. Through this awareness and associated strategies, educators are more comfortable juggling the learning phases. They create colourful capsules to best suit everyone's preferences. Advances in neuroscience research are challenging many false beliefs about learning.

2. Connection: Move towards the learners
Motivation is "the love of learning, the love of challenge" and is more important than initial capacity because it determines success. It creates a developmental and successful mindset in students that brings and maintains commitment. Therefore, through active listening, identifying and removing obstacles to motivation is a priority. A promising way to achieve this is to create co-development dynamics for a stimulating and engaging partnership between educators, parents, and students.

3. Curiosity: From Teaching to Facilitation
Curiosity (head, heart, body) plays a key role in the learning process by placing the learner in a state of high receptivity. To develop it, an iterative and collaborative approach is to be favoured. It should therefore

be given a large place in the learning sessions. Since the well-being and performance of pupils is linked to the educator's pedagogy, the major objective for the educator is to facilitate as much pedagogical autonomy in their learning as possible. But it is still necessary to know how to question, listen, and provide effective feedback. The hybrid approach that combines face-to-face and distance learning fully meets today's expectations for engagement.

4. Confidence: From Concentration to Success
It is not enough to put students in front of a task and expect them to acquire knowledge and skills. How can they learn if they don't know how to learn?[87] To fully engage in learning, they need to have confidence. Reflective metacognitive activities in the classroom that examine how we process our thoughts and emotions play an important role in building that confidence and in developing learning strategies. Respectful interactions make these metacognition activities fruitful. Awareness and reflection on one's own ways of learning, confronted with those of one's peers, leads students to develop and enrich their strategies. However, these classroom metacognition activities only have real impact if educators themselves have confidence in each student's success.

5. Communication: From Sharing Our Strengths to Success
Interactions promote learning, as shown by Ph. Dessus and E. Gentaz.[88] Developing interactions between students that are respectful of

---

87   J.M. Zakhartchouk, Apprendre à apprendre.

88   Ph. Dessus and E. Gentaz, Apprentissage et enseignement: Sciences cognitives et éducation.

methodological and communication preferences will encourage greater involvement in learning. The content exchanged helps learners discover multiple ways of learning that become rich in promises of progress for everyone. The multiplication of interactions and the creation of support constellations makes students more accountable and provides them with the energy they need for their efforts: motivation and success to get them on the right track!

Conclusion

All learners are curious and eager to exploit their unlimited potential. It is an absolute joy to be an educator when you're able to reach your learners and unlock this curiosity and eagerness. By combining proven pedagogical approaches, advances in neuroscience, and research in behavioural psychology, we can show them the way to this potential. What a dream for both educator and learner! Today, it is possible to create attractive and efficient learning paths that will lead students to greater autonomy, development, and success. Thanks to an enlightened use of new technologies, blended learning offers courses whose attractiveness engages learners more easily and everywhere in the world. However, we need to adapt and engage in a more comprehensive learning approach to keep up with this modern world.

Every educational context is an experiential space, and we should strive to foster positive physical and virtual interactions. These interactions are further facilitated through curious questioning and introspection as well as a clear and agile how-to-learn model at home, at school, and online. This model presents an invitation to learning which allows collaborative connections to emerge and blossom. These learning experiences can be imperfect and open-ended but still fruitful; when students and educators are aligned, the learners become the experts. In order for this to occur, a more personal learning process is required.

> *"To be able to know yourself better, you have to be able to imagine yourself."*
> **Gianni Rodari**

By imagining their way of learning, by connecting awareness to behaviour, and by interacting with learners in a co-designed context and content, students will be guided by educators to access their own powerful learning tools, to be more confident, motivated, and resourceful learners. Mind-agile learners will interact with themselves and others as they embark on a life-long learning journey. This journey of shared and true interactions is like a new encounter between two co-authors. It is a relationship that co-emerges and co-exists through empathy and honesty.

I was born in France and at the age of 11, I wanted to be a spy... but instead, I decided to go on a passionate training-facilitating-coaching career in seven different countries, within companies, international schools, and the French Ministry of Foreign Affairs. Then, my spying career caught up with me! I decided to spy on the learning brain and dig deeper into the *Learning How to Learn* process. I discovered how our brains work and how emotion and cognition are related. I also discovered how the social aspects of our learning journeys are essential. My dream became to bring a language to the forefront that can bridge home, school, and online learning.

Today I design conferences, workshops and experiential learning capsules (social, emotional, and metacognitive) as a consultant for schools (European School II, French School in Luxembourg, private schools in Paris, École Montessori Schule Hobsheid, École Eau Vive) and companies (Caceis, JP Morgan, Know Futures).

If, like me, you have the same dream and would like to know more about the engaging Agility of Mind approach on how to develop it at home, at school, at work, or online, don't hesitate to reach out to me through Facebook or LinkedIn, or send me a message: contact@sophieledorner.com

Summary

We live in a world of rapid change where the entire educational system is constantly challenged by more and more administrative tasks taking time away from teaching; the mastery of distance learning overnight; no real partnership between parents and teachers; a lack of learning culture within the school; the need for actionable, concrete, and efficient pedagogical approaches; and the lack of recognition of and support for teachers facing the complexity of the world of learning.

The Agility of Mind is a learner-centred approach that creates interactions, guiding learners towards confident learning in which they can fully engage and consciously embrace change. Being aware of the reality of the complexity of a classroom, and the diversity of learning dynamics outside the classroom, the *Agility of Mind* approach is open to everything that facilitates concrete interactive practices. It is inspired, among other things, by the contributions of the cognitive sciences, behavioural sciences, neuropedagogy, and positive psychology. It helps to facilitate the educational path at school, at home, and online, and it is easy to implement.

The Agility of Mind allows learners to discover and develop their ways of learning; on the other hand, it provides educators as well as parents with the means to support learners as closely as possible to their needs.

It does this by:

- Promoting the use of a common language for clear communication between children, parents, and educators.

- Multiplying positive collaborative experiences to encourage each learner to actively engage.

- Developing metacognition activities for lifelong learning minds.

- Taking into account the rhythms and preferences of each learner at home, at school, and online.

- Developing a curious mind to deal with the complexity of reality.

- Focusing on the acquisition of soft skills easily embedded in the curriculum.

Sophie Le Dorner presents a collaborative inquiry model that allows educators to actually achieve what they always wanted: a more engaging learning outcome through collective efficacy that can be implemented step by step. It includes sharing a common language as a collaborative device and an intuitive signposted approach in colours to engage learning autonomy and bring the ecosystem together. Educators will discover five easy steps: consciousness, connection, curiosity, confidence, and communication, the 5Cs to make learning engagement at school, at home, and online easy to implement. This approach requires small, actionable changes to create big changes.

Let's all create learning interactions through an *Agility of Mind!*

www.ingramcontent.com/pod-product-compliance
Lightning Source LLC
Chambersburg PA
CBHW040415100526
44588CB00022B/2830